Brothers Christian

Primary Arithmetic

mental and written New series

Brothers Christian

Primary Arithmetic
mental and written New series

ISBN/EAN: 9783337300289

Printed in Europe, USA, Canada, Australia, Japan

Cover: Foto ©Andreas Hilbeck / pixelio.de

More available books at **www.hansebooks.com**

PRIMARY

ARITHMETIC

MENTAL AND WRITTEN

NEW SERIES

BY THE

BROTHERS OF THE CHRISTIAN SCHOOLS

---

46 SECOND STREET, NEW YORK

1887

Electrotyped by
E. Harmer Smith & Sons.

Printed by
Alexander Anderson.

CONTENTS.

PREFACE.

THIS Primary Arithmetic, though not an integral part of our New Series, forms, nevertheless, an important introduction to the science of numbers. Its object is to supply young pupils with a convenient book of exercises on the four fundamental operations.

Its matter is not purely suggestive ; nor, on the other hand, is its scope too extensive. It does not pretend to replace the living teacher. A primary arithmetic, like all other text-books, should be adapted to the wants of the class-room. Its aim should be the complete mastery of the elements of numbers. "One thing at a time," "accuracy rather than rapidity," should be its guiding principle. In it the teacher should find ample and suitable material for exercising his pupils upon every combination of the fundamental rules.

Having been planned and arranged according to this standard, we hope that the present little book will prove a valuable assistant to teachers in their efforts to develop the minds of youth.

PRIMARY ARITHMETIC.

NUMERATION AND NOTATION.

1. *Numeration* is the method of reading numbers.

2. *Notation* is the method of writing numbers.

3. Numbers are expressed by the following ten

Figures: 1, 2, 3, 4, 5, 6, 7, 8, 9, 0.
Names: One, Two, Three, Four, Five, Six, Seven, Eight, Nine, Naught.

4. The number which follows the ninth is called *ten*. It is represented by writing the figure 1 with a naught after it ; thus, 10.

EXERCISES.

Read and write each of the following numbers :

1 2 3 4 5 6 7 8 9 10

5. The next numbers in order are :

Eleven,	11.	Fifteen,	15.
Twelve,	12.	Sixteen,	16.
Thirteen,	13.	Seventeen,	17.
Fourteen,	14.	Eighteen,	18.
	Nineteen,	**19.**	

NOTE.—The "teen" in the words thirteen, etc., to nineteen, means *ten*. So that, strictly speaking, thirteen means three and ten; fourteen, four and ten, etc.

EXERCISES.

Read and write the following numbers:

11 12 13 14 15 16 17 18 19

Write the figures for:

Three.	Six.	Seven.	Sixteen.	Fourteen.	Nineteen.
Five.	Eight.	Ten.	Thirteen.	Fifteen.	Eighteen.
Two.	Naught.	Nine.	Twelve.	Seventeen.	Fourteen.
Four.	Eleven.	One.	Eighteen.	Sixteen.	Thirteen.

Write the names of:

4.	7.	8.	15.	19.	11.
2.	9.	6.	17.	12.	16.
5.	1.	0.	10.	18.	15.
3.	7.	4.	13.	14.	19.

6. We count by tens as we count by simple units, saying: *one ten, two tens, three tens, nine tens.* But custom has replaced these words by the following:

Twenty,	20.	Sixty,	60.
Thirty,	30.	Seventy,	70.
Forty,	40.	Eighty,	80.
Fifty,	50.	Ninety,	90.

NOTE.—The "ty" in these words signifies ten.

7. The numbers between twenty and thirty, between thirty and forty, etc., are expressed as follows:

Twenty-one,	21.	Thirty-one, etc.,	31, etc.
Twenty-two,	22.	Forty-one, etc.,	41, etc.
Twenty-three,	23.	Fifty-one, etc.,	51, etc.
Twenty-four,	24.	Sixty-one, etc.,	61, etc.
Twenty-five,	25.	Seventy-one, etc.,	71, etc.
Twenty-six,	26.	Eighty-one, etc.,	81, etc.
Etc.		Ninety-one, etc.	91, etc.

The highest number expressed by two figures being ninety-nine, 99.

EXERCISES.

I.

Write the numbers between :

Thirty and Forty.	Sixty and Seventy.
Forty and Fifty.	Seventy and Eighty.
Fifty and Sixty.	Eighty and Ninety.

Ninety and Ninety-nine.

II.

Copy and read the following numbers, naming the *tens* and *units* in each :

1.	*2.*	*3.*	*4.*	*5.*	*6.*	*7.*	*8.*
17	28	55	53	85	29	70	73
12	26	22	87	44	10	89	98
11	30	37	62	33	61	64	72
16	90	48	32	67	99	23	27
13	79	40	43	97	21	14	58
37	69	31	34	79	33	74	80
46	59	19	50	60	54	82	49
39	12	83	78	96	86	95	92
20	91	75	68	51	71	19	41

III.

Express the following numbers by figures :

1. Ten.	*9.* Eighty-six.	*17.* Seventy-six.
2. Thirty-seven.	*10.* Ninety-eight.	*18.* Sixty-eight.
3. Seventeen.	*11.* Thirteen.	*19.* Eighteen.
4. Fifty-eight.	*12.* Forty-five.	*20.* Forty-four.
5. Forty-three.	*13.* Thirty-six.	*21.* Sixteen.
6. Twenty-one.	*14.* Forty-seven.	*22.* Seventy.
7. Forty-two.	*15.* Eleven.	*23.* Nineteen.
8. Twenty-three.	*16.* Ninety-seven.	*24.* Twelve.

25. Twenty-six.	*33.* Eighty.	*41.* Eighty-three.
26. Seventy-one.	*34.* Twenty-four.	*42.* Fifty-six.
27. Fifty-one.	*35.* Thirty-seven.	*43.* Fifty-nine.
28. Sixty-three.	*36.* Sixty-two.	*44.* Seventy-eight.
29. Thirty-nine.	*37.* Twenty.	*45.* Forty-six.
30. Fifty.	*38.* Twenty-eight.	*46.* Sixty-three.
31. Fifteen.	*39.* Forty.	*47.* Ninety-two.
32. Seventy-nine.	*40.* Sixty.	*48.* Eighty-seven.

8. The number which follows ninety-nine (99) is called *hundred.* It is represented by writing 1 with two naughts after it ; thus, 100.

9. We count by hundreds as we count by units, saying :

One hundred,	100.	Five hundred,	500.
Two hundred,	200.	Six hundred,	600.
Three hundred,	300.	Seven hundred,	700.
Four hundred,	400.	Eight hundred,	800.

Nine hundred, 900.

10. The names of the numbers included between two consecutive hundreds, are formed by joining, successively, to the name of the first of these hundreds, the names of all the numbers less than one hundred; thus,

One hundred one,	101.	Two hundred eleven,	211.
One hundred two,	102.	Three hundred twelve,	312.
One hundred three,	103.	Four hundred thirteen,	413.
One hundred four,	104.	Five hundred fourteen,	514.
One hundred five,	105.	Six hundred fifteen,	615.
One hundred six,	106.	Seven hundred sixteen,	716.
One hundred seven,	107.	Eight hundred seventeen,	817.
One hundred eight,	108.	Nine hundred eighteen,	918.
One hundred nine,	109.	One hundred nineteen,	119.
One hundred ten,	110.	Two hundred twenty,	220.

Three hundred thirty-one, 331.
Four hundred forty-two, 442.
Five hundred fifty-three, 553.
Six hundred sixty-four, 664.
Seven hundred seventy-five, 775.
Eight hundred eighty-six, 886.
Nine hundred ninety-seven, 997.
Nine hundred ninety-eight, 998.

Nine hundred ninety-nine (999) is the highest number that can be expressed by three figures.

EXERCISES.

1.

Copy and read the following numbers, naming the *hundreds*, *tens*, and *units* in each:

1.	2.	3.	4.	5.	6.
100	509	224	861	652	278
211	256	297	598	720	122
121	905	337	250	862	972

7.	8.	9.	10.	11.	12.
700	840	103	305	722	605
306	273	110	606	465	334
426	590	733	467	533	407
900	406	892	850	573	863
640	634	920	670	798	580
723	777	701	999	877	121
572	308	620	202	346	313
248	407	800	706	723	816
309	863	462	501	244	911

II.

Express the following numbers in figures :

1. Three hundred seventy-six.
2. Nine hundred sixty-eight.
3. Five hundred forty-three.
4. Six hundred eighty-four.
5. Six hundred twenty-three.
6. Nine hundred eighty-three.
7. Eight hundred twenty-three.
8. Five hundred ninety-five.
9. Three hundred forty-seven.
10. One hundred thirty-eight.
11. Two hundred fifty-two.
12. Nine hundred sixty-one.
13. Four hundred ninety-seven.
14. Nine hundred eighty-two.
15. Three hundred forty-five.
16. Seven hundred nine.
17. Eight hundred two.
18. Five hundred seventy-two.
19. Seven hundred two.
20. Six hundred fifty-four.

21. One hundred seventy.

22. Three hundred twenty-nine.

23. Nine hundred nine.

24. Six hundred five.

25. Seven hundred sixty.

26. Four hundred seventy.

27. Three hundred twenty-seven.

28. Five hundred ninety-seven.

29. Four hundred ninety.

30. Two hundred eighty-four.

31. Four hundred seventy-five.

32. Seven hundred seven.

33. Seven hundred seventy.

34. Eight hundred eighty.

35. Five hundred sixty-one.

36. Nine hundred ninety-nine.

37. Three hundred thirty-three.

11. The number which follows 999 is called *thousand*, and is represented by writing the figure 1 with three naughts after it ; thus, 1000.

The units of thousands are :

One thousand,   two thousand, ... nine thousand.
    1000,   2000,   9000.

The tens of thousands are :

Ten thousand,   twenty thousand,... ninety thousand.
    10000,   20000,   90000.

The hundreds of thousands are :

One hundred thousand,   two hundred thousand,
    100000,   200000,
.... nine hundred thousand.
       900000.

EXERCISES.

I.

Copy and read the following numbers:

1.	*2.*	*3.*	*4.*	*5.*	*6.*
1831	1030	9184	2040	2983	8899
4785	2686	1025	3107	3174	5580
7340	1522	2222	5043	4065	1001
6837	7403	6807	7041	7831	2050
8001	· 5465	5273	7856	4563	3307
8788	1401	6600	4624	4000	3009
2027	6434	1020	4862	5980	2010
1456	8573	5409	4709	1036	3008

II.

7.	*8.*	*9.*	*10.*	*11.*
15462	63041	68489	25738	71392
21009	79825	73401	10506	59989
30450	38678	39632	81911	63009
78921	10909	71854	12134	24784
44333	80006	27374	10096	87004

III.

12.	*13.*	*14.*	*15.*	*16.*
442839	905497	634584	251206	990098
756351	680329	100091	358192	431960
296426	751341	390400	876538	829473
807905	608315	745001	704115	110018
431900	917823	370492	171211	980703
272861	189966	258633	151616	224455
112595	404050	179481	929284	703020
781620	309980	557733	406070	807733

I.

Express in figures the following :

1. One thousand, eight hundred eighty-two.
2. Three thousand, nine hundred four.
3. Two thousand, nine.   Six thousand, eight.
4. One thousand, eight hundred sixty-three.
5. Seven thousand, five hundred forty-one.
6. Nine thousand, forty-seven.   Five hundred five.
7. Six thousand, three hundred eighty-four.
8. Nine thousand, one hundred twenty-seven.
9. Six thousand, five hundred eighty-nine.
10. Three thousand, one hundred five.
11. One thousand, one hundred twenty-two.
12. One thousand, three hundred fifty-five.
13. Eight thousand, eight hundred ninety-seven.
14. Six thousand, three hundred forty.
15. Eight thousand, eight hundred ninety-six.
16. Four thousand, eight hundred seventy-one.
17. Five thousand, six.   Nine thousand, fifty.
18. Three thousand, nine hundred forty-five.
19. Eight thousand, thirty.   Four thousand, four.
20. Two thousand, nine hundred eighty-seven.

II.

21. Thirty-one thousand, two hundred.
22. Seventy thousand, eighty-four.
23. Eighty-seven thousand, six.
24. Ten thousand, one.   Seven thousand, two.
25. Twenty thousand, two hundred two.
26. Fifteen thousand, eight hundred forty.
27. Twelve thousand, three hundred seventeen.
28. Twenty-five thousand, eight hundred nine.

29. Sixty-three thousand, seven hundred one.

30. Forty-four thousand, nine hundred sixty-three.

31. Seventy-six thousand, eight hundred ten.

32. Ninety-nine thousand, four hundred twenty-five.

33. Eighty-six thousand, nine hundred ninety-nine.

34. Sixty-one thousand, two. Sixty thousand.

35. Ten thousand, ten. Fifteen thousand.

III.

36. Eight hundred six thousand, nine hundred seven.

37. Five hundred twenty-seven thousand, eight hundred two. Nine hundred twelve thousand.

38. Six hundred twenty-five thousand, nine hundred.

39. Six hundred twelve thousand, one hundred thirty-six. One hundred thousand, twenty-six.

40. Nine hundred thousand, six.

41. One hundred twenty-one thousand, three hundred nineteen. Five hundred ten thousand.

42. Eight hundred thousand.

43. Eight hundred twenty-five thousand, eight.

44. Six hundred eleven thousand, ninety-four.

45. Nine hundred forty thousand, thirty.

46. Eight hundred nine thousand.

47. One hundred sixty-one thousand, seven hundred eighty-four. Three hundred twenty thousand.

48. Three hundred ninety-one thousand, two hundred eleven. Nine hundred eighty-two thousand.

49. One hundred ninety-nine thousand, nine hundred ninety-nine. Two hundred six thousand.

50. Six hundred forty-four thousand, nine hundred.

12. Continuing in the same manner, we form the next higher periods, *Millions, Billions, Trillions,* etc.

13. For convenience in reading and writing numbers, the figures are divided into *periods,* each of which comprises three places. The *first three* places constitute the *first,* or *units'* period ; the second three places constitute the *second,* or *thousands'* period ; etc.

14. This division of the periods will be easily seen from the following

NUMERATION TABLE.

NAMES OF ORDERS.	Hundreds of Trillions.	Tens of Trillions.	Units of Trillions.	Hundreds of Billions.	Tens of Billions.	Units of Billions.	Hundreds of Millions.	Tens of Millions.	Units of Millions.	Hundreds of Thousands.	Tens of Thousands.	Units of Thousands.	Hundreds.	Tens.	Units.
NAMES OF PERIODS.	Trillions,			Billions,			Millions,			Thousands,			Units.		
NUMBER.	840			625			074			503			040		
ORDERS.	15th	14th	13th	12th	11th	10th	9th	8th	7th	6th	5th	4th	3d	2d	1st
PERIODS.	5th			4th			3d			2d			1st		

15. If it be required to read or write numbers above trillions, the following is the order of some of the next higher periods : *Quadrillions, Quintillions, Sextillions, Septillions, Octillions,* etc.

What number is expressed by 82135249 ?

SOLUTION.—Beginning at the right, separate these figures into periods of three figures each; thus, 82,135,249. As shown in the table, the third period is *millions*, the second *thousands*, and the first *units*. Hence, the number is 82 millions, 135 thousands, and 249 units.

NOTES.—1. In reading, the pupil should say, eighty-two million, one hundred thirty-five thousand, two hundred forty-nine.

2. If an order, or even an entire period, be wanting, we do not mention it. We also omit to name the last, or units' period, because it is understood.

Read the following numbers :

1.	*2.*	*3.*	*4.*	*5.*	*6.*	*7.*
83	39	157	865	219	327	210
96	52	291	917	998	890	414
75	14	605	324	632	600	300
43	76	310	417	551	402	650
71	28	877	668	703	170	881
87	64	186	539	999	534	576

8.	*9.*	*10.*	*11.*	*12.*
1234	8207	3302	2323	8008
2591	1090	1708	9998	7009
8163	6400	5006	1111	1314
5075	2016	7000	4342	8594
4810	8984	3000	8673	2452
6494	7609	4100	1481	1606
2819	2234	1202	2537	6760
1007	1908	1515	5863	3890
1208	1415	3018	3341	1752
1030	2404	4162	8090	3587

13.	14.	15.	16.	17.
27136	80132	35256	79000	61621
40094	18078	19416	26310	83097
11208	55804	35324	31078	15100
50371	73497	72563	27350	70060

18.	19.	20.	21.	22.
421312	101080	890036	400008	999111
362110	200060	700000	506002	709002
570341	809073	810750	310721	550660
895006	150730	600000	611819	211322
170003	581672	212092	430534	677006

23.	24.	25.	26.
2198765	5482200	1405060	2390086
3779843	9180406	8300009	1515156
3200670	4706204	7000015	3040605
7064021	7601036	1200130	2723074
5623103	4706203	8070904	1182212

27.	28.	29.	30.
23782621	60300001	18998410	31500004
48631425	72060384	29357639	90088050
77666555	10010010	14986371	60500281
43125789	83000505	17884635	40730800
52706000	18009130	27809410	29394900

31.	32.	33.	34.
900010210	709080062	978564123	842900601
122299880	203100000	806273871	120340560
151461711	840601007	552118622	400300600
506040300	320000006	486374628	910004576
102030000	786400200	111222333	800006301

35.	*36.*	*37.*
8493726150	12304710916	603091121810
7036407984	44022334592	365042874908
1110033706	12140870632	478763000060
1581915567	57159482419	213056017317
7323138796	80603356917	590070005600

EXERCISES IN NOTATION.

1. Express in figures the number *three* million, two hundred ten thousand, four hundred fifty-six.

SOLUTION.—This number consists of three periods, *millions*, *thousands*, and *units*. As there are only three millions, write the figure 3 in units of millions' place.

In thousands' period there are two hundreds, one ten, and no units. Write, therefore, in this period, the figure 2 in hundreds' place, the figure 1 in tens' place, and the figure 0 in units' place.

Lastly, in units' period, write the figure 4 in hundreds' place, the figure 5 in tens' place, and the figure 6 in units' place. Hence, the figures 3210456, are the proper expression for the given number.

I.

Express the following numbers in figures :

2. Fifteen. Twelve. Twenty. Eighteen.

3. Seventeen. Twenty-six. Sixty-three. Thirty.

4. Forty-four. Eighty-seven. Fifty. Sixty-one.

5. Ninety-eight. Thirty-nine. Forty-four. Seventy.

6. Sixty-six. Eighty-five. Forty. Thirty-five.

7. Seventy-six. Fifty-eight. Thirty-three. Eighty.

8. Twenty-three. Thirty-six. Sixty. Forty-nine.

9. One hundred seven. One hundred eighteen.

10. Four hundred eleven. Three hundred sixty-two.

11. Two hundred ten. Six hundred twenty-one.

12. Seven hundred twenty-two. Five hundred nine.

13. Eight hundred fifty-nine. Six hundred forty.
14. Six hundred eighty. Two hundred thirty-four.
15. Nine hundred ten. Five hundred sixty-seven.
16. Four hundred fifty-three. One hundred ninety.
17. Eight hundred eighty. Nine hundred twelve.
18. Four hundred four. Three hundred thirty-four.
19. One hundred seventy-one. Six hundred thirty.
20. Five hundred seventy-three. Eight hundred ten.
21. Nine hundred fifty-eight. Four hundred sixty.
22. Three hundred twenty. Seven hundred seventeen.
23. Seven hundred ninety-nine. Two hundred eleven.
24. Three hundred nineteen. Two hundred forty.
25. Six hundred six. Five hundred twenty-five.

II.

26. Eight thousand, six hundred fifty-eight.
27. Two thousand, one hundred eighty-seven.
28. Nine thousand, three hundred seventy-five.
29. One thousand, seven hundred nineteen.
30. Six thousand, four hundred thirty-nine.
31. Four thousand, nine hundred ninety-eight.
32. Three thousand, five hundred forty-two.
33. Seven thousand, four hundred.
34. Five thousand, eight hundred two.
35. Six thousand, two hundred nine.
36. Eight thousand, three hundred.
37. Nine thousand, eighteen.
38. Seven thousand, two hundred three.
39. Four thousand, two. One thousand, five.
40. Nine thousand, twelve. Two thousand, eight.
41. Six thousand, forty. Nine thousand, thirty-one.
42. One thousand, four hundred seventy-four.
43. Five thousand, one hundred thirteen.

44. Two thousand, fourteen.   Nine thousand, three.
45. Four thousand, twenty.   Six thousand, fifty.

III.

46. Fifteen thousand, one hundred thirty-one.
47. Sixteen thousand, two hundred forty-five.
48. Eleven thousand, three hundred thirty-three.
49. Nineteen thousand, four hundred six.
50. Twelve thousand, six hundred two.
51. Ten thousand, ten.   Seven thousand, three.
52. Thirteen thousand.   Eight thousand, thirteen.
53. Seventeen thousand.   Three thousand, six.
54. Twenty thousand, twenty.   Six thousand, two.
55. Forty-one thousand, two hundred thirty-four.
56. Twenty thousand, four hundred nine.
57. Forty-one thousand, five hundred sixty.
58. Thirty-nine thousand, seven hundred two.
59. Eighty-four thousand, two hundred eight.
60. Seventy-one thousand, thirty.   One thousand, one.

IV.

61. One hundred thousand, three hundred.
62. Two hundred thousand, five hundred six.
63. Six hundred thousand, nine hundred ten.
64. Nine hundred twelve thousand, two hundred six.
65. Three hundred four thousand, one hundred two.
66. Eight hundred sixty-one thousand, fourteen.
67. One hundred fifty-three thousand, nine hundred seventy-five.   Two hundred thirty thousand.
68. Two hundred twelve thousand, eight hundred sixty-nine.   Five hundred six thousand.
69. Seven hundred twenty-two thousand, ninety-six.
70. Four hundred one thousand, twenty-five.

71. Nine hundred thousand. Four hundred two thousand. Nine hundred three thousand.

72. Three hundred thousand, one hundred.

73. Seven hundred three thousand, five hundred nine.

74. Four hundred thousand, four. Five hundred thousand. Nine hundred thousand, six.

75. One hundred sixteen thousand, four hundred twelve.

V.

76. Four million, six hundred ten thousand, four hundred ninety-nine.

77. Nine million, eight hundred twenty-two thousand, seven hundred four.

78. Six million, nine hundred thousand, one hundred seventy-five. Five million, seven hundred thousand.

79. Eight million, twelve thousand, sixty.

80. Seven million, sixteen thousand, forty.

81. Ten million, three thousand, seventy-one.

82. Fifteen million, two hundred three thousand, six hundred. Eight million, six hundred four thousand.

83. Seventeen million, eight hundred thousand, five hundred six. Nine million, three hundred nine thousand.

84. Twenty-four million, twelve thousand, ninety.

85. Forty-one million, seven thousand, thirty.

86. Eighty-six million, three hundred thousand, one hundred. Seventy-six million, two hundred thousand.

87. Fifty-four million. Sixty-eight million, nine thousand, twenty. Forty-six million, twenty.

88. Sixty-five million, thirty-two thousand, twenty-one. Fifty-seven million, forty-four thousand.

89. Twenty-nine million, one hundred seventy thousand, four hundred sixty-two.

90. Two hundred eighteen million, nine hundred forty-six thousand, three hundred ninety-four.

91. Seven hundred twenty million, nine hundred twelve thousand, two hundred thirty-five.

92. Six hundred seven million, forty-two thousand, fifty. Three hundred nine million, ten thousand.

93. One hundred million, two hundred thousand, three hundred. Three hundred million, six thousand.

94. Nine hundred sixty million, four thousand, forty.

95. Four hundred ten million, six hundred thousand, two hundred. Two hundred five million, one thousand.

96. Thirteen million, one thousand, twenty.

97. Sixty million, seven. Five million, three.

98. Eighteen million, nine. Three hundred million, thirty. Six million, nine hundred thirty-three.

99. Three billion, eleven million, ten thousand, eighty.

100. One hundred twenty billion, fourteen million, ten thousand, seventy-one.

101. Two hundred fifty-seven billion, nine million, sixty-four thousand, forty-two.

102. Four hundred thirty-two billion, ninety million, three thousand, twenty-five.

103. Six hundred seventy-six billion, two hundred fifty-six million, seventy-four thousand, sixty-seven.

104. Six billion, nine million, two thousand, forty-six.

105. Ninety-four billion, one hundred seventy-nine million, sixty-five thousand, four hundred eighty-three.

106. Seventy-nine billion, ninety-seven million, three hundred forty-four thousand, twenty-eight.

107. Six hundred fifty-six million, eight hundred forty-two thousand, seven hundred ninety-nine.

108. Eight hundred ninety-six billion, forty-five million, nine thousand, eight hundred forty-one.

ADDITION.

16. *Addition* is the method of finding a single number that is equal to two or more given numbers put together.

ILLUSTRATION.—To find the sum of 5 and 4, we proceed as follows: 4 is the sum of 1, 1, 1, and 1. Adding each of these ones in succession, to 5, we have 5 and 1 are 6, 6 and 1 are 7, 7 and 1 are 8, 8 and 1 are 9; that is, the two given numbers, 5 and 4, are equal to the single number 9.

ADDITION TABLE.

0 and any number make that number: 0 and 1 are 1; 0 and 2 are 2.
Any number and 0 make that number: 1 and 0 are 1; 2 and 0 are 2.

1 and 1 are 2	6 and 1 are 7	8 and 3 are 11
2 and 1 are 3	6 and 2 are 8	8 and 4 are 12
2 and 2 are 4	6 and 3 are 9	8 and 5 are 13
3 and 1 are 4	6 and 4 are 10	8 and 6 are 14
3 and 2 are 5	6 and 5 are 11	8 and 7 are 15
3 and 3 are 6	6 and 6 are 12	8 and 8 are 16
4 and 1 are 5	7 and 1 are 8	9 and 1 are 10
4 and 2 are 6	7 and 2 are 9	9 and 2 are 11
4 and 3 are 7	7 and 3 are 10	9 and 3 are 12
4 and 4 are 8	7 and 4 are 11	9 and 4 are 13
5 and 1 are 6	7 and 5 are 12	9 and 5 are 14
5 and 2 are 7	7 and 6 are 13	9 and 6 are 15
5 and 3 are 8	7 and 7 are 14	9 and 7 are 16
5 and 4 are 9	8 and 1 are 9	9 and 8 are 17
5 and 5 are 10	8 and 2 are 10	9 and 9 are 18

I.

How many are :

2 and 1 ?	4 and 1 ?	1 and 1 ?	6 and 4 ?
1 and 8 ?	3 and 4 ?	5 and 6 ?	8 and 8 ?
3 and 1 ?	3 and 0 ?	4 and 5 ?	7 and 8 ?
0 and 4 ?	6 and 3 ?	5 and 4 ?	5 and 3 ?
5 and 2 ?	7 and 2 ?	1 and 9 ?	9 and 7 ?
2 and 2 ?	4 and 4 ?	7 and 3 ?	4 and 8 ?
3 and 2 ?	0 and 2 ?	6 and 2 ?	0 and 6 ?
6 and 1 ?	9 and 4 ?	3 and 9 ?	2 and 8 ?
4 and 2 ?	3 and 8 ?	5 and 7 ?	9 and 6 ?
8 and 0 ?	0 and 1 ?	7 and 6 ?	8 and 5 ?

II.

What is the sum of :

3 + 3 ?	9 + 8 ?	2 + 3 ?	4 + 7 ?
7 + 4 ?	9 + 9 ?	3 + 4 ?	7 + 8 ?
9 + 2 ?	5 + 0 ?	5 + 8 ?	4 + 9 ?
6 + 8 ?	0 + 3 ?	6 + 9 ?	1 + 8 ?
0 + 7 ?	7 + 1 ?	6 + 7 ?	2 + 6 ?
4 + 0 ?	6 + 6 ?	4 + 6 ?	3 + 5 ?
7 + 7 ?	7 + 9 ?	3 + 8 ?	2 + 7 ?
5 + 1 ?	0 + 9 ?	5 + 5 ?	2 + 9 ?
9 + 5 ?	3 + 6 ?	7 + 0 ?	0 + 8 ?
8 + 9 ?	4 + 8 ?	5 + 6 ?	5 + 9 ?

III.

1. 6 bats and 3 bats are how many bats ?

2. 4 boys and 5 boys are how many boys?

3. 7 dollars and 2 dollars are how many dollars ?

4. 2 cents and 5 cents are how many cents?

5. 4 girls and 3 girls are how many girls?

6. 7 houses and 5 houses are how many houses ?

7. 5 fishes and 8 fishes are how many fishes ?

8. 9 tops and 1 top are how many tops ?

9. A boy paid 1 cent for a stick of candy and 2 cents for an apple ; how many cents did both cost ?

SOLUTION.—If a stick of candy cost 1 cent, and an apple cost 2 cents, both must cost the sum of 1 cent and 2 cents. The sum of 1 cent and 2 cents is 3 cents. Therefore, both cost 3 cents.

10. John's father gave him two apples, and his mother gave him two more ; how many apples had John then ?

11. George had 4 chestnuts and Joseph gave him 3 ; how many had George then ?

12. If a pencil cost 2 cents, and a copy 6 cents, how many cents will both cost ?

13. William lost 7 marbles and has 6 remaining ; how many had he at first ?

14. There are 8 birds on one tree, and 9 on another ; how many birds on both trees?

15. There are 4 hens in one coop, and 5 in another ; how many hens in both coops ?

16. I travelled 4 miles one day, and 7 miles the next ; how many miles did I travel in both days ?

17. There are 6 eggs in one nest, and 8 in another ; how many eggs in both nests ?

18. Paid 5 cents for a kite, and 9 cents for some string ; how much did both cost ?

19. A man bought 3 horses on Wednesday, and 9 on Saturday ; how many horses did he buy ?

20. James put 8 chairs in the parlor, and 6 in the kitchen ; how many chairs did he put in the two rooms ?

21. Michael bought 8 marbles, and afterwards won 7 ; how many marbles had he then ?

IV.

Tell sums at sight:

	1st.	2d.	3d.	4th.	5th.	6th.	7th.	8th.	9th.
A. {	4	3	0	2	1	5	2	3	4
	7	9	6	8	9	6	9	0	8
B. {	2	1	3	5	5	8	6	8	2
	4	2	8	4	0	3	2	1	0
C. {	1	9	7	8	7	6	7	2	3
	1	5	7	8	0	8	9	1	4
D. {	4	1	2	4	2	4	6	5	9
	2	3	7	1	2	0	4	5	3
E. {	1	3	7	4	5	4	9	3	7
	4	6	6	9	1	8	1	5	2
F. {	6	7	4	7	1	8	6	9	2
	1	3	6	8	7	6	5	4	1
G. {	8	0	3	4	7	6	6	4	9
	2	2	7	3	5	6	7	1	6
H. {	6	3	5	7	2	3	9	0	1
	3	1	7	4	3	3	2	1	6
I. {	0	4	8	0	1	4	5	3	2
	3	4	5	5	8	5	3	2	5
J. {	2	1	5	6	3	6	5	8	1
	6	0	2	9	2	0	9	4	5
K. {	9	3	1	9	2	8	4	9	8
	8	5	9	0	8	7	6	9	7

V.

Add :

1. 1 and 0, 10 and 3, 20 and 5, 30 and 7, 40 and 9.

2. 51 and 2, 61 and 4, 71 and 6, 81 and 9, 91 and 0.

3. 2 and 1, 12 and 1, 22 and 2, 32 and 2, 42 and 3.

4. 53 and 3, 63 and 4, 73 and 4, 83 and 5, 93 and 5.

5. 4 and 6, 14 and 6, 24 and 7, 34 and 7, 44 and 0.

6. 55 and 0, 65 and 8, 75 and 8, 85 and 9, 95 and 9.

7. 6 and 9, 16 and 8, 26 and 7, 36 and 6, 46 and 5.

8. 97 and 0, 87 and 1, 77 and 2, 67 and 3, 57 and 4.

9. 8 and 7, 18 and 3, 28 and 6, 38 and 8, 48 and 4.

10. 69 and 1, 59 and 0, 79 and 9, 89 and 2, 99 and 5.

11. 71 and 8, 54 and 2, 78 and 4, 60 and 6, 3 and 53.

12. 82 and 7, 34 and 6, 83 and 7, 9 and 99, 2 and 88.

13. 25 and 8, 37 and 7, 5 and 45, 3 and 30, 54 and 8.

14. 31 and 7, 42 and 6, 30 and 7, 61 and 8, 89 and 3.

VI.

Write the following with answers :

$21+9=?$	$64+3=?$	$91+9=?$	$63+9=?$	$92+7=?$
$13+6=?$	$72+5=?$	$21+8=?$	$78+6=?$	$86+3=?$
$24+1=?$	$60+7=?$	$7+14=?$	$53+9=?$	$72+9=?$
$42+6=?$	$34+9=?$	$93+7=?$	$82+6=?$	$6+12=?$
$35+9=?$	$88+4=?$	$46+5=?$	$9+31=?$	$7+99=?$
$74+8=?$	$62+9=?$	$13+8=?$	$8+12=?$	$55+2=?$
$56+6=?$	$57+8=?$	$40+0=?$	$90+7=?$	$93+9=?$
$47+7=?$	$63+5=?$	$61+8=?$	$68+13=?$	$27+6=?$
$11+8=?$	$23+9=?$	$32+1=?$	$49+7=?$	$7+84=?$
$65+7=?$	$33+8=?$	$57+5=?$	$49+9=?$	$6+26=?$
$91+4=?$	$41+9=?$	$82+8=?$	$19+8=?$	$5+39=?$
$83+8=?$	$65+8=?$	$96+3=?$	$27+6=?$	$8+47=?$
$75+7=?$	$74+9=?$	$68+6=?$	$55+3=?$	$4+86=?$

VII.

Tell sums at sight :

	1.	*2.*	*3.*	*4.*	*5.*	*6.*	*7.*	*8.*	*9.*
A.	9	9	9	9	9	9	9	9	9
	40	80	70	50	20	10	30	60	90
B.	9	9	9	9	9	9	9	9	9
	51	61	31	41	71	91	21	81	11
C.	9	9	9	9	9	9	9	9	9
	42	52	92	72	32	12	62	22	82
D.	9	9	9	9	9	9	9	9	9
	13	33	93	73	43	83	53	23	63

NOTE.—These exercises are intended to illustrate a very important blackboard drill. The method is as follows: the teacher has all the numbers, from 10 to 99, arranged as indicated above. Over each of them he places one of the nine digits, and has the pupils announce the sums at sight. When the pupils can give the totals rapidly and in any order whatever, the teacher should change the digit for another.

VIII.

Add :

1. By threes, from 2 to 110. Thus, 2 and 3 are 5, and 3 are 8, and 3 are 11, etc.

2. By twos, from 3 to 81. From 5 to 49.

3. By threes, from 1 to 61. From 7 to 37.

4. By fours, from 3 to 115. From 1 to 81.

5. By fives, from 2 to 77. From 3 to 78.

6. By fives, from 4 to 104. From 8 to 58.

7. By sixes, from 3 to 57. From 1 to 55.

8. By sixes, from 5 to 83. From 7 to 37.

9. By sevens, from 4 to 116. From 2 to 58.

10. By sevens, from 6 to 118. From 9 to 100.
11. By eights, from 1 to 89. From 3 to 91.
12. By eights, from 5 to 69. From 6 to 126.
13. By eights, from 7 to 55. From 12 to 132.
14. By nines, from 3 to 102. From 2 to 101.
15. By nines, from 4 to 76. From 8 to 125.
16. By nines, from 8 to 116. From 10 to 118.
17. By threes, from 11 to 44. From 19 to 49.
18. By fives, from 7 to 47. From 16 to 61.
19. By sevens, from 9 to 86. From 12 to 96.

IX.

A.			B.			C.		
1st.	2d.	3d.	1st.	2d.	3d.	1st.	2d.	3d.
0	0	0	0	2	0	0	2	0
0	1	1	2	2	1	3	3	1
0	1	0	2	2	2	3	3	2
0	1	1	2	2	0	3	3	3
0	1	0	2	2	1	3	3	0
0	1	1	2	2	2	3	3	1
0	1	0	2	2	0	3	3	2
0	1	1	2	2	1	3	3	3
0	1	0	2	2	2	3	3	0
0	1	1	2	2	0	3	3	1
0	1	0	2	2	1	3	3	2
0	1	1	2	2	2	3	3	3
0	1	0	2	2	0	3	3	0
0	1	1	2	0	1	1	3	1

NOTES.—1. In adding these exercises, the pupil should mention only the results. Thus, in the 3d column of division C, he should say: 1, 4, 6, 7, 10, 12, 13, 16, 18, 19.

2. No advancement should be made until the pupils can add with rapidity and accuracy what goes before.

D.

1st.	2d.	3d.	4th.
0	2	4	0
4	4	4	1
4	4	4	2
4	4	4	3
4	4	4	4
4	4	4	0
4	4	4	1
4	4	4	2
4	4	4	3
4	4	4	4
4	4	4	0
4	4	4	1
4	4	4	2
1	3	4	3

E.

1st.	2d.	3d.	4th.
0	2	4	0
5	5	5	1
5	5	5	2
5	5	5	3
5	5	5	4
5	5	5	5
5	5	5	0
5	5	5	1
5	5	5	2
5	5	5	3
5	5	5	4
5	5	5	5
5	5	5	0
1	3	5	1

F.

1st.	2d.	3d.	4th.	5th.
0	2	4	6	0
6	6	6	6	1
6	6	6	6	2
6	6	6	6	3
6	6	6	6	4
6	6	6	6	5
6	6	6	6	6
6	6	6	6	0
6	6	6	6	1
6	6	6	6	2
6	6	6	6	3
6	6	6	6	4
6	6	6	6	5
1	3	5	6	6

G.

1st.	2d.	3d.	4th.	5th.
0	2	4	6	0
7	7	7	7	1
7	7	7	7	2
7	7	7	7	3
7	7	7	7	4
7	7	7	7	5
7	7	7	7	6
7	7	7	7	7
7	7	7	7	0
7	7	7	7	1
7	7	7	7	2
7	7	7	7	3
7	7	7	7	4
1	3	5	7	5

	H.						I.				
1st.	2d.	3d.	4th.	5th.	6th.	1st.	2d.	3d.	4th.	5th.	6th.
0	1	3	5	7	0	0	2	4	6	8	0
8	8	8	8	8	1	9	9	9	9	9	1
8	8	8	8	8	2	9	0	9	9	9	2
8	8	8	8	8	3	9	0	9	9	9	3
8	8	8	8	8	4	9	9	9	9	9	4
8	8	8	8	8	5	9	0	9	9	9	5
8	8	8	8	8	6	9	9	0	9	9	6
8	8	8	8	8	7	9	9	9	9	9	7
8	8	8	8	8	8	9	9	9	9	9	8
8	8	8	8	8	0	9	9	9	9	9	9
8	8	8	8	8	1	9	9	9	9	9	0
8	8	8	8	8	2	9	9	9	9	9	1
8	8	8	8	8	3	9	9	9	0	9	2
8	2	4	6	8	4	1	3	5	7	9	3

					J.					
1st.	2d.	3d.	4th.	5th.	6th.	7th.	8th.	9th.	10th.	11th.
8	2	7	9	8	7	6	0	3	1	9
7	9	5	8	4	9	5	4	9	6	7
5	6	4	6	1	0	1	0	2	4	4
4	4	9	0	9	2	8	2	1	8	3
3	0	2	9	2	8	7	8	6	0	1
2	1	7	7	0	7	6	9	0	8	0
0	3	8	5	0	9	7	5	8	7	9
8	9	0	3	5	1	2	3	9	6	5
6	7	5	0	7	5	0	8	7	8	6
7	8	6	7	6	4	4	5	8	3	2
5	5	9	4	9	8	6	9	3	0	8
8	2	8	8	7	3	2	6	4	5	7
4	8	3	5	8	6	9	2	8	2	3
9	6	4	3	5	7	5	8	7	6	9

X.

1. A newsboy sold 10 papers in the morning and 7 in the afternoon. How many papers did he sell during the day?

2. If Joseph has 3 cents in one pocket, and 10 cents in another, how many cents has he?

3. William paid 12 cents for a slate, and 1 cent for a pencil. What did he pay for both?

4. There are 17 trees in one field, and 9 in another. How many trees in the two fields?

5. If there are 15 panes of glass in one window, and 8 in another, how many panes in both windows?

6. Francis had 25 cents, and his uncle gave him 5 more. How many cents had Francis then?

7. Albert took 14 roses from a bush, and Mary took 9 from the same bush. How many roses were taken from the bush?

8. If John say 64 words in a minute, and Thomas 8, how many words will both say in a minute?

9. Thomas plucked 47 plums from a tree, and picked 9 off the ground. How many plums had Thomas?

10. In a company there are 56 private soldiers, and 6 officers. How many men in the company?

11. How many cents must I pay for a pound of butter worth 36 cents, and a pound of cheese worth 9 cents?

12. Robert having 65 marbles, won 8. How many had he then?

13. There are 19 books on a shelf and 6 on a table. How many books in all?

14. During a recitation, 25 questions were answered correctly and 8 incorrectly. How many questions were asked?

XI.

Give sums at sight :

68	42	57	54	39	24
10	25	30	45	60	75

57	31	68	43	47	18
11	26	31	56	61	86

46	29	79	32	38	38
12	27	42	57	62	87

35	92	81	29	47	59
13	38	43	58	73	98

24	80	72	38	66	62
24	39	44	59	74	99

32	67	19	27	45	54
41	14	93	86	63	75

Give sums at sight :

20 + 30.	30 + 90.	10 + 67.	49 + 20.
50 + 40.	70 + 40.	30 + 85.	83 + 30.
60 + 80.	60 + 50.	90 + 24.	68 + 50.
20 + 90.	40 + 20.	60 + 72.	29 + 40.
60 + 40.	90 + 80.	50 + 96.	34 + 80.
70 + 50.	70 + 60.	20 + 84.	65 + 70.
10 + 60.	80 + 60.	90 + 27.	72 + 50.
20 + 80.	70 + 70.	80 + 63.	87 + 80.
90 + 30.	20 + 60.	50 + 47.	55 + 30.
50 + 60.	10 + 90.	60 + 82.	62 + 90.
30 + 70.	40 + 50.	30 + 75.	81 + 60.
80 + 40.	80 + 70.	40 + 36.	44 + 70.

XII.

Find the sum of :

10 and 16.	44 and 16.	32 and 47.	28 and 39.	92 and 18.
25 and 11.	24 and 36.	25 and 27.	76 and 54.	87 and 32.
36 and 13.	73 and 38.	62 and 37.	67 and 58.	19 and 91.
12 and 27.	17 and 57.	17 and 92.	44 and 63.	80 and 57.
14 and 40.	28 and 15.	73 and 73.	71 and 28.	26 and 90.
62 and 12.	39 and 32.	64 and 48.	88 and 15.	80 and 40.
47 and 10.	46 and 27.	49 and 56.	12 and 63.	47 and 52.
28 and 21.	22 and 25.	91 and 27.	29 and 34.	77 and 67.
16 and 33.	83 and 45.	47 and 68.	56 and 33.	54 and 98.
37 and 12.	44 and 67.	61 and 92.	16 and 16.	67 and 99.

XIII.

1. William has 54 cents, and James has 43. How much money have both?

2. A farmer having 47 ducks, bought 16 more. How many ducks did he have then?

3. How many dollars will pay for a shawl worth 27 dollars, and a dress worth 45 dollars?

4. A butcher killed 25 cows on one day, and 38 the next day. How many cows did he kill on both days?

5. A tailor sold 75 yards of cloth on Monday, and 62 yards on Tuesday. What was the amount sold?

6. Purchased two tubs of butter, the larger containing 93 pounds, and the smaller 56 pounds. How much butter did I purchase?

7. A real estate agent sold two lots containing, one, 83 acres, and the other, 44. How many acres did he sell?

8. In a school consisting of two classes, the first class has 42 pupils, and the second 71. How many pupils in the school?

9. A man owes 35 dollars for groceries, and 72 dollars for rent. How much does he owe?

10. Henry is now 16 years of age. How old will he be 36 years hence?

11. Jane's library contains 35 books, and Charles's 25. How many books in both libraries?

12. John received 33 good points for arithmetic one week, and 38 the next. How many good points did he receive in both weeks?

13. Patrick gave 75 cents for an Advanced Reader, and 55 cents for a small dictionary. How much did he give for both?

14. In a certain class 26 boys have red neckties, and the remainder, 17 boys, have blue neckties. How many boys in the class?

15. During a monthly competition, one class received 93 credits, and another 78. How many credits were received by both?

16. How much money will be required to purchase a bat worth 65 cents, and a ball worth 80 cents?

17. Andrew bought a pair of skates for 95 cents, and sold them so as to gain 16 cents. What was his selling price?

18. February has 28 days and March 31. How many days in both months?

19. A tailor sold 46 yards of cloth to Mr. Smith, and 39 to Mr. Jones. How many yards of cloth did he sell?

20. If I pay $28 for 35 yards of cloth, for what must I sell it to gain $1 on each yard?

21. A farmer sold a wagon for $57, and a sleigh for $43. How much did he receive for both?

22. Henry shot 29 birds, and Andrew shot 36. How many birds did both shoot?

OPERATION OF ADDITION.

What is the sum of 708, 926, and 387 ?

OPERATION.

708
926
387
————
2021

SOLUTION.—Beginning with units, add each column separately. The sum of 7 units, 6 units, and 8 units is 21 units, or 2 tens and 1 unit. Put the 1 unit under units' column, and carry the 2 tens to tens' column. 2 tens, 8 tens, and 2 tens equal 12 tens, or 1 hundred and 2 tens. Placing the 2 tens under tens' column, carry the 1 hundred to hundreds' column.

1 hundred, 3 hundreds, 9 hundreds, and 7 hundreds make 20 hundreds, which, put under hundreds' column, gives the complete answer, 2021.

NOTES.—1. When adding, the pupil should mention only the results; thus, 7, 13, 21.

2. In order to prove that the work is correct, each column should be added downwards.

WRITTEN EXERCISES.

I.

1.	2.	3.	4.	5.	6.	7.
475	507	272	426	587	648	557
204	492	129	457	107	239	227

8.	9.	10.	11.	12.	13.	14.
123	456	789	647	777	435	575
567	234	209	125	113	445	405

15.	16.	17.	18.	19.	20.	21.
807	347	545	476	576	746	427
184	528	429	114	117	149	239

22.	23.	24.	25.	26.	27.	28.
574	247	·176	379	486	596	149
219	389	277	485	297	279	288

29.	30.	31.	32.	33.	34.	35.
279	374	489	547	187	276	357
185	384	265	274	284	185	168

36.	37.	38.	39.	40.	41.	42.
489	577	345	456	748	679	574
257	194	456	265	285	178	279

43.	44.	45.	46.	47.	48.	49.
457	705	345	496	896	576	897
754	804	189	794	944	647	409

50.	51.	52.	53.	54.	55.	56.
507	354	805	320	609	·456	517
493	497	495	407	769	832	491

57.	58.	59.	60.	61.	62.	63.
621	707	424	524	617	779	475
724	797	397	415	493	776	794

II.

1.	2.	3.	4.	5.	6.
232	314	603	456	572.	921
345	530	415	301	101	608
524	321	562	450	536	75

7.	8.	9.	10.	11.	12.
176	674	715	335	643	496
302	523	672	856	129	257
490	241	805	274	576	490

13.	*14.*	*15.*	*16.*	*17.*	*18.*
739	815	192	377	970	734
103	700	31	168	473	309
75	367	900	440	550	843
270	110	216	688	237	515

19.	*20.*	*21.*	*22.*	*23.*	*24.*
849	94	280	709	392	206
23	252	331	821	780	760
681	30	439	67	61	397
322	809	72	346	907	685

III.

1.	*2.*	*3.*	*4.*	*5.*
3416	7422	6089	6780	7230
8743	8674	7906	3007	1691
2655	9830	4078	5944	7425

6.	*7.*	*8.*	*9.*	*10.*
2937	1809	1870	9384	1924
7315	2375	9780	1286	4357
1630	1505	1515	3164	1443
1790	1304	1917	1350	1291

11.	*12.*	*13.*	*14.*	*15.*
8912	3965	1045	7432	1009
7056	2138	3923	5631	4982
2398	4760	7864	8476	3875
1702	9023	5231	9401	4623
4109	8197	2109	7198	9742
4915	6380	2062	6594	6308
3598	4700	3172	7831	5132

IV.

1. 93 + 137 + 205.		*13.* 924 + 315 + 796.
2. 379 + 977 + 182.		*14.* 190 + 75 + 134.
3. 143 + 297 + 388.		*15.* 521 + 134 + 650.
4. 157 + 388 + 651.		*16.* 175 + 171 + 99.
5. 438 + 166 + 876.		*17.* 84 + 300 + 907.
6. 183 + 477 + 265.		*18.* 219 + 10 + 85.
7. 981 + 774 + 332.		*19.* 30 + 506 + 231.
8. 392 + 605 + 19.		*20.* 73 + 165 + 294.
9. 149 + 876 + 544.		*21.* 812 + 27 + 60.
10. 136 + 709 + 832.		*22.* 100 + 480 + 200.
11. 153 + 186 + 703.		*23.* 742 + 812 + 665.
12. 98 + 134 + 820.		*24.* 898 + 767 + 353.

V.

Add the following :

1. Three hundred ninety ; eight hundred thirty-six ; three hundred twenty-six ; and two hundred nine.

Ans. 1761.

2. Three thousand, forty-eight ; one thousand, four hundred eighteen ; one thousand, two hundred fifty-two ; and one thousand, nine hundred ninety-one.

Ans. 7709.

3. Eight hundred two ; two hundred seventy-two ; two hundred sixteen ; and five hundred thirty-nine.

Ans. 1829.

4. Six hundred ten ; one thousand, seven hundred thirty-six ; four thousand, eight hundred ninety-seven ; seven hundred one ; eight hundred thirty-three ; and seven hundred ninety-six. *Ans.* 9573.

5. One thousand, two hundred two ; five thousand, five hundred five ; six hundred seventy-eight ; two thousand, fifty-one ; and one thousand, three hundred thirty-nine.   *Ans.* 10775.

6. Two thousand, three hundred sixty-seven ; eight hundred seven ; five hundred twenty-four ; and three thousand, one hundred seventy.   *Ans.* 6868.

7. Four thousand, five hundred seventy-eight ; nine hundred sixty-one ; five hundred seventy-two ; and three hundred sixty-three.   *Ans.* 6474.

8. One thousand, three hundred nine ; four thousand, three hundred twenty-nine ; one thousand, two hundred sixty-five ; three hundred eight ; and four hundred twenty-six.   *Ans.* 7637.

9. Eight hundred ; four thousand, one hundred eighty-three ; two thousand, one hundred sixty-four ; three hundred twenty ; and eight hundred five.

10. Four hundred thirty ; nine hundred twenty-three ; eight hundred two.

11. Seven hundred ninety-two ; two hundred sixty-seven ; five hundred eighty-one.

12. Eight hundred seventy-nine ; four hundred forty-one ; one hundred one.

13. Two hundred ; five hundred three ; nine hundred eighty-seven.

14. Thirty-seven ; six hundred ninety-four ; three hundred forty-one.

15. One thousand, two hundred seventy-five ; six thousand, nine hundred four ; two thousand, four hundred twenty-two ; three thousand, seven hundred ninety-four.

16. Seven thousand, four hundred seventy ; two thousand, three hundred eighty-five ; nine thousand, twenty ; four thousand, six hundred ninety-one.

17. Six thousand, three hundred sixty-six ; one thousand, nine hundred eighty-one; four thousand, six hundred twenty-four; five thousand, one.

18. Three thousand, one hundred four; five thousand, six hundred thirty-one; one thousand, nine hundred eighty-three; eight thousand, four hundred seventy-eight.

19. Nine thousand, four; six thousand, three hundred sixty-three; eight thousand, seven hundred forty-one; one thousand, nine hundred ten.

VI.

1.	2.	3.	4.	5.
40331	66432	38765	27301	99863
16979	71811	44581	95172	28243
14114	37728	3082	38677	72137

6.	7.	8.	9.	10.
80603	73612	90205	37145	86744
43766	24903	10377	10280	11920
12298	68108	34861	79164	61914
16481	19348	88709	8107	99467

11.	12.	13.	14.	15.
96327	37951	56789	99777	89174
86438	98029	37454	66888	30200
69476	96746	15079	55444	75588

16.	17.	18.	19.	20.
333355	45706	509234	76815	66644
766988	569897	767448	274867	91359
544375	847687	189979	537967	75248

VII.

1. Three hundred sixty-five thousand, four hundred sixty-two; five hundred sixty thousand, four hundred twenty-seven; four hundred five thousand, seven hundred sixty-three; one hundred thirty-six thousand, one hundred sixty-six. *Ans.* 1467818.

2. Three hundred twenty; four hundred fourteen thousand, five hundred ninety; and eight hundred seventy. *Ans.* 415780.

3. Two thousand, five hundred thirty-seven; nine thousand, three hundred eighty-one; six hundred sixty-eight; nine hundred; and fifty-nine thousand, seven hundred forty-four. *Ans.* 73230.

4. Seven hundred three; one thousand, five hundred ninety; one hundred twenty; eight hundred thousand, sixty-six; and three thousand, seven hundred seventy-seven.

5. Two hundred ten thousand, three hundred eight; twenty-eight thousand, seven hundred fifty-six; three thousand, one hundred forty-two; and thirteen thousand, seven hundred fifty.

6. One hundred nineteen thousand, ninety-four; two hundred three thousand, six hundred four; two hundred fifty-five thousand, two hundred seventeen; three hundred thousand, sixty-five; and sixty-eight thousand, six hundred. *Ans.* 946580.

7. Sixty-four thousand, four hundred sixty-seven; one thousand, five hundred twenty; seven thousand, nine hundred thirty-six; thirteen thousand, seven hundred forty-four; nine thousand, nine hundred fifty-five; and eleven thousand, eight hundred twenty-two.

8. Twenty-eight thousand, five hundred twenty-two;

seventy-four thousand, three hundred forty-four; nine hundred twenty-nine; seventy thousand, nine hundred seven; eighty-three thousand, four hundred three; forty-three thousand, seven hundred ninety-four.

9. Thirty-four thousand, six hundred ninety-one; forty-three thousand, seven hundred twenty-two; one hundred five thousand, sixty-four; two hundred sixty-four thousand, nine hundred seventy-seven; eight hundred forty-nine thousand, two hundred thirty-four.

10. Seven hundred forty-one; nine thousand, one hundred seventy-two; thirty-two thousand, seven hundred ninety-three; one hundred seventy-one thousand, three hundred one; fifty-six thousand, four hundred eighty-seven; seven hundred forty-three thousand, nine hundred eighty-one.

11. Two hundred sixty-three thousand, five hundred five; three hundred ninety-four thousand, four hundred ninety-one; seven hundred thirteen thousand, six hundred fifteen; seven thousand, eight hundred two; three hundred forty-six thousand, one hundred nine; four hundred seventy-three thousand, seven hundred ninety-four.

12. One hundred eighteen thousand, four hundred sixteen; three hundred forty-nine thousand, four hundred sixty-five; nine hundred twenty-one thousand, seven hundred eighteen; seven hundred thirty-two; eight hundred thousand, two hundred.

13. Seventy-three thousand, seven hundred twenty-five; one hundred ninety-five thousand, three hundred twenty-seven; three hundred twenty-one; thirty-eight thousand, two hundred forty-five; eighty-five thousand, seven hundred ninety-eight; thirty-three thousand, three hundred.

VIII.

1.	*2.*	*3.*	*4.*	*5.*
205	910	749	102	482
431	796	322	893	396
304	804	416	421	410
276	510	702	605	516
153	312	512	734	503
236	908	762	417	954

6.	*7.*	*8.*	*9.*	*10.*
4321	6893	5002	8192	7893
5678	405	3015	3050	4821
3134	7931	6912	600	5632
5063	3144	7896	75	345
2093	5689	4004	9144	21
7245	3965	7965	842	4002
2653	201	4689	5000	3112
1644	6354	4135	215	9900
3091	2947	7486	9931	6750

11.	*12.*	*13.*	*14.*	*15.*
9132	4562	6486	2345	9784
4216	3954	2447	2981	4956
5842	1894	5819	7108	3927
7720	9467	1234	5643	5273
8654	5974	9768	2731	1459
9328	3192	3521	1852	2186
1217	1804	7923	2946	1355
5689	5287	4210	1598	9761
1181	1718	8816	7584	2775
6012	3600	3350	5614	6676

IX.

1.	2.	3.	4.	5.	6.
125	530	215	490	327	748
214	471	425	175	721	624
344	127	679	382	218	219
679	899	119	567	917	356
406	676	742	996	627	654
302	504	899	455	482	737
544	334	677	874	824	828
634	965	321	325	935	919
782	427	709	751	359	415
999	306	798	982	539	542

7.	8.	9.	10.	11.
695	499	2016	8210	8452
126	709	4959	5739	1690
481	870	8734	6214	3007
184	482	6759	8009	654
322	940	897	1691	783
441	309	789	3040	1310
562	206	989	2757	2534
491	466	8653	1620	982

12.	13.	14.	15.	16.
57531	91065	59008	42035	14183
470	7767	8222	14399	1001
6343	2030	11795	8700	250
8898	18019	4479	4432	13000
7987	27400	6319	1110	25009
20498	886	20881	5989	14141
5375	9949	3162	74843	962
9473	7820	43785	62358	7006

17.	*18.*	*19.*	*20.*	*21.*
65781	38393	20301	89329	10300
94975	97684	89734	72013	1201
70897	37469	50632	40965	900
84518	54567	39217	81708	60000
39572	92841	40982	34562	8006
64784	91950	56721	93149	300
43062	86372	24002	99825	70705
14849	59841	96831	42623	4800
39047	61136	44765	18764	79
28634	90410	51384	56348	28003

X.

Add by lines :

1. $385 + 771 + 366 + 2004 + 5087.$
2. $879 + 4682 + 456 + 2808 + 7864 + 697.$
3. $408 + 4684 + 476 + 656795 + 630.$
4. $824 + 378 + 557 + 2097 + 6848.$
5. $29008 + 64329 + 2647 + 981 + 4825.$
6. $7935 + 10880 + 96145 + 1285 + 990 + 140705.$ ·
7. $395489 + 6887897 + 687985514 + 73846702.$
8. $4717 + 3667454 + 53496243 + 276435318.$
9. $994 + 868 + 919 + 7422 + 8688 + 4110 + 973 + 80.$
10. $984275 + 587965 + 665989 + 67201 + 8604 + 79.$
11. $635 + 4376 + 987 + 6487 + 3028 + 356 + 7085 + 467.$
12. $4605 + 89670 + 76548 + 45308 + 4697 + 38409 + 98.$
13. $75436 + 89 + 486 + 53719 + 43652 + 1785 + 69857.$
14. $4398 + 48657 + 658 + 34968 + 7865 + 497 + 21503.$
15. $567453 + 781 + 5934 + 85436 + 87 + 647 + 816649.$
16. $868909 + 74753 + 972565 + 8864 + 687596 + 809.$
17. $8835 + 777 + 666407 + 95608 + 897545 + 53454.$ ·
18. $97 + 5678 + 80957 + 683474 + 809 + 184265 + 707.$

19. 11 + 222 + 3333 + 44444 + 555555 + 666 + 777 + 88.
20. 4186374 + 8426 + 70931 + 86 + 708 + 33674 + 707.
21. 457987 + 7684 + 89090 + 9000 + 48 + 198 + 4394.
22. 764989 + 8000146 + 14823605 + 97856 + 4063.
23. 76757 + 80321 + 17 + 840 + 33786 + 70643217 + 10.
24. 687306891 + 82730 + 100706 + 203 + 1234 + 5678.

UNITED STATES CURRENCY.

17. The *Sign,* **$,** written before a number, signifies *dollars.* Thus, the expression $120 is read *one hundred twenty dollars.*

18. *Dollars* and *cents* may be written together, the *cents* being separated from the *dollars* by a point. Thus, the expression $25.35 is read 25 *dollars* and 35 *cents.*

WRITTEN EXERCISES.

Express, by proper signs and figures, the following:

1. Four dollars and thirty-nine cents.
2. Twelve dollars and twenty-two cents.
3. Sixty-four dollars and seventy-five cents.
4. Eighty-one dollars and ten cents.
5. Fifteen cents. Thirty-seven cents. Eleven cents.
6. Fifty cents. Forty-five cents. Sixteen cents.
7. Twenty-eight cents. 'Forty-three cents.
8. Thirteen dollars and sixteen cents.
9. Thirty-six dollars and fifty-six cents.
10. Eighty-four dollars and ninety-two cents.
11. Sixty-eight dollars and eleven cents.
12. Twenty-three dollars and forty-eight cents.
13. Ninety-three dollars and sixty-two cents.
14. Forty-one dollars and twenty-eight cents.
15. Eighty-four dollars and twenty-nine cents.

16. Fifty-one dollars and nineteen cents.
17. Three cents. Nine cents. Twenty-five dollars.
18. Thirty-four cents. Seventy-nine cents.
19. Twenty-eight cents. Fourteen cents.
20. Thirty-eight cents. Seventy cents.

19. In writing dollars and cents for the purpose of adding them, the separating points must stand in the same column.

WRITTEN EXERCISES.

I.

1.	2.	3.	4.	5.
$2.70	$9.15	$5.00	$1.03	$7.14
4.20	2.70	2.05	2.07	9.20
.25	3.22	8.21	3.50	.87
1.53	5.17	9.73	4.19	1.32
.63	.29	5.91	7.48	8.19
$9.31				

6.	7.	8.	9.
$113.12	$24.15	$34.16	$19.02
223.17	212.89	323.15	633.10
39.43	416.24	62.30	875.00
574.15	729.20	125.75	238.95

10.	11.	12.
$50203.15	$87420.18	$13250.95
7832.24	73286.70	38032.17
13917.75	45840.73	25893.16
1835.29	68773.25	14315.56
2030.64	39340.40	470290.42
7490.50	94839.85	536520.18

13.	14.	15.	16.
$2115.64	$2900.10	$108.79	$9800.17
3908.23	23.02	2000.00	1503.70
2247.15	107.23	187.13	15.27
1326.35	1479.92	2009.89	2308.93
5374.93	8430.75	9773.60	7570.10
1073.03	2200.03	207.10	256.48

17. Find the sum of $75.85 ; $16.05 ; $123.25 ; $475 ; $325.50 ; $110.16.

18. Fihd the sum of $3284.63 ; $87.24 ; $1325.55 ; $1806.10.

19. Add $26.45 ; $33.80 ; $70.67 ; $8.70 ; and $63.73.

20. Add $135.10 ; $0.17 ; $1.67 ; $1800 ; $3.60 ; and $867.25.

21. A grocer bought sugar for $19.27 ; coffee for $8.35 ; tea for $16.75 ; butter for $17.16 ; cheese for $5.70 ; and eggs for $4.75. What was the amount of his purchases?
Ans. $71.98.

22. A owes $137.75 to B ; $297.25 to C ; $960 to D ; and $500.50 to E. What is his indebtedness to these four persons ?

23. A lady purchased a dress for $27.60 ; a shawl for $14.75 ; a bonnet for $6.50 ; a pair of gloves for $1.75 ; and 6 handkerchiefs for 90 cents. How much money did she thus expend ?
Ans. $51.50.

24. Mr. Owens bought a house for $3816 ; paid $175.75 for repairing it, and $200.75 for painting it ; he then sold it at a profit of $575.50. What was his selling price ?
Ans. $4768.

25. A merchant imported goods to the amount of $3827.50 ; paid duties $650.75 ; and freight $127.50. What was the entire cost of the goods ?

26. A farmer made the following sales : wheat $687 ; potatoes $67 ; corn $180.75 ; cabbage $16.80 ; turnips $20.60 ; apples $76.05 ; pears and peaches $99.18. What was the amount of the sales ?

27. How much will a pupil pay for the following set of school-books : Intermediate Reader 45 cents ; Grammar 36 cents ; Arithmetic 40 cents ; Catechism 12 cents ; Geography 70 cents ; and a U. S. History 25 cents ?

Ans. $2.28.

In the following exercises, add both by columns and by lines :

1. Sales of a Book Store.

	Mon.	Tues.	Wed.	Thurs.	Fri.	Sat.	Total.
Papers......	789	1032	1204	1360	2500	1934	*****
Magazines..	362	439	1107	836	1223	907	*****
Fiction.....	380	734	226	319	163	231	*****
Science.....	131	215	258	112	342	371	*****
Poetry......	92	115	173	411	103	145	*****
Religion....	104	397	339	483	127	240	*****
Total.....	*****	*****	*****	*****	*****	*****	*****

2. Mail at a City Post Office.

	Mon.	Tues.	Wed.	Thurs.	Fri.	Sat.	Total.
Ordinary Letters	8417	7343	7911	8010	9370	8176	*****
Registered "	934	652	420	501	216	123	*****
Postal Cards....	2004	2619	2304	2779	3012	2651	*****
Books..........	732	840	530	798	831	792	*****
Packages.......	253	211	403	95	90	398	*****
Papers..........	14970	1323	1975	1031	1481	17243	*****
Total........	*****	*****	*****	*****	*****	*****	*****

3. Cash Receipts.

	Mon.	Tues.	Wed.	Thurs.	Fri.	Sat.	Total.
First Week......	$231.12	$69.74	$289.17	$145.60	$8.42	$120.00	*****
Second Week....	72.26	121.12	65.39	834.84	16.73	12.35	*****
Third Week......	4.12	898.80	181.99	606.00	10.12	401.63	*****
Fourth. Week....	3.92	87.00	900.50	57.00	301.06	66.60	*****
Fifth Week.....	10.42	9.08	74.00	717.70	69.80	32.11	*****
Sixth Week.....	181.00	75.05	82.92	8.64	107.98	600.74	*****
Seventh Week....	96.84	641.08	6.04	14.50	274.06	58.05	*****
Eighth Week....	7.27	837.19	58.14	46.92	3.25	292.00	*****
Ninth Week.....	18.18	.99	793.96	523.33	.76	9.40	*****
Total	*****	*****	*****	*****	*****	*****	*****

4. Sales of a Grocery Store.

	Tea.	Coffee.	Sugar.	Flour.	Butter.	Cheese.	Total.
January........	142	197	1589	4830	730	342	*****
February........	129	204	1232	932	1036	503	*****
March..........	136	308	1937	873	2130	783	*****
April...........	141	1037	994	3002	1098	1009	*****
May	138	936	1637	5738	1230	1138	*****
June..........	143	707	2990	4860	1573	997	*****
July	120	1037	2001	3200	1381	1097	*****
August.....	1311	2034	3652	939	1450	932	*****
September......	1023	1329	2036	3937	1560	1030	*****
October.........	1403	939	2840	9300	1495	1116	*****
November.......	903	1023	2340	2463	1562	1234	*****
December.	1007	1325	2798	2830	1343	1287	*****
Total..........	*****	*****	*****	*****	*****	*****	*****

5. A Contractor's Expenses.

	Jan.	Feb.	Mar.	April.	May.	June.	Total.
First Section...	$1820.00	$980.00	$970.50	$1450.00	$1321.00	$1515.00	*****
Second Section.	968.22	760.14	831.19	990.43	1008.00	1109.00	*****
Third Section..	654.10	673.56	710.29	784.23	900.00	941.61	*****
Fourth Section.	341.09	561.00	781.00	621.11	730.00	798.40	*****
Fifth Section ..	221.31	360.98	390.00	410.16	508.00	501.05	*****
Sixth Section...	183.96	43.72	98.80	154.68	129.14	190.22	*****
Seventh Section	94.70	100.01	280.10	190.16	75.48	107.91	*****
Eighth Section.	941.61	730.00	410.16	98.80	100.01	154.68	*****
Total...	*****	*****	*****	*****	*****	*****	*****

WRITTEN EXERCISES.

1. Henry was born in the year 1872. In what year will he be 46 years of age ?   *Ans.* 1918.

2. What is the weight of three bales of cotton, weighing, respectively, 475, 686, and 592 pounds ?
          Ans. 1753 pounds.

3. A regiment of cavalry has 558 horses in the first squadron, 390 in the second, and 480 in the third. How many horses in the regiment ?   *Ans.* 1428 horses.

4. What are the expenses of a gentleman who lays out $360 for furniture, $482 for clothing, and $690 for provisions ?   *Ans.* $1532.

5. The population of a certain village in 1850 was 2460 souls. The next year it gained 341 ; the next 864 ; the next 425 ; and the next 274. What was its population in 1854 ?   *Ans.* 4364.

6. A boy bought an arithmetic for 85 cents, a grammar for 70 cents, a geography for $2.25, a piece of India rubber for 4 cents, and a lead pencil for 3 cents. What did he spend ?

7. If William can count 3896 in one hour, how many can he count in four hours ?

8. A merchant bought a quantity of silk for $649, and a quantity of cloth for $836. What did both cost ?

9. A grocer paid $1275 for flour, $1647 for salt-pork, $1207 for beef, and $647 for butter. How much did he pay for all ?

10. A school is divided into five classes. The first contains 36 pupils ; the second 50 ; the third 70 ; the fourth 97 ; and the fifth 130. How many pupils in the school ?

11. If a lot were purchased for $15780, and a house

built upon it at a cost of $10856, and both sold at a profit of $2863, how much was received for them ?

> *Ans.* $29499.

12. In an orchard there are 257 cherry trees, 563 apple trees, 86 pear trees, and 54 plum trees. How many trees in the orchard ?

13. A fort was bombarded from three different places. From the first 3486 shots were fired ; from the second, 3547 ; and from the third, 4927. What was the number of shots fired ?   *Ans.* 11960 shots.

14. Bought a pair of boots for $7.50, a hat for $4.25, a pair of suspenders for $.65, an umbrella for $2.75, and a pair of gloves for $1.37. What was the whole cost ?

15. Mr. Somers paid $3500 for a farm, $357 for cattle, $409.50 for hay, and $225.75 for improvements. What were his expenses ?

16. A freight train, from Buffalo to New York, was loaded with 5286 bushels of wheat, 3792 bushels of oats, 4963 bushels of rye, and 7932 bushels of barley. How many bushels of grain on the train ?

17. A lumber dealer sold 16283 feet of pine boards, 13965 feet of hemlock, 4967 feet of ash, and 349 feet of mahogany. How many feet of lumber did he sell in all ?

18. A produce dealer bought 627 bushels of potatoes, 257 bushels of onions, 835 bushels of corn, 1233 bushels of wheat, and 489 bushels of turnips. How many bushels in all did he buy ?

19. A dry-goods merchant paid $625.30 for silk, $248.90 for calico, $503.75 for cloth, and $897.20 for woolen goods. What were his expenses ?

20. Richard won 98 marbles the first week, 103 the second week, 59 the third week, and 78 the fourth week. How many marbles in all did he win ?

SUBTRACTION.

20. *Subtraction* is the method of finding what number is left when a smaller number is taken from a greater.

SUBTRACTION TABLE.

0 from any number leaves that number; thus, 0 from 1 leaves 1; 0 from 2 leaves 2, etc.

1 from 1 leaves 0	2 from 2 leave 0	3 from 3 leave 0
1 from 2 leaves 1	2 from 3 leave 1	3 from 4 leave 1
1 from 3 leaves 2	2 from 4 leave 2	3 from 5 leave 2
1 from 4 leaves 3	2 from 5 leave 3	3 from 6 leave 3
1 from 5 leaves 4	2 from 6 leave 4	3 from 7 leave 4
1 from 6 leaves 5	2 from 7 leave 5	3 from 8 leave 5
1 from 7 leaves 6	2 from 8 leave 6	3 from 9 leave 6
1 from 8 leaves 7	2 from 9 leave 7	3 from 10 leave 7
1 from 9 leaves 8	2 from 10 leave 8	3 from 11 leave 8
1 from 10 leaves 9	2 from 11 leave 9	3 from 12 leave 9

4 from 4 leave 0	5 from 5 leave 0	6 from 6 leave 0
4 from 5 leave 1	5 from 6 leave 1	6 from 7 leave 1
4 from 6 leave 2	5 from 7 leave 2	6 from 8 leave 2
4 from 7 leave 3	5 from 8 leave 3	6 from 9 leave 3
4 from 8 leave 4	5 from 9 leave 4	6 from 10 leave 4
4 from 9 leave 5	5 from 10 leave 5	6 from 11 leave 5
4 from 10 leave 6	5 from 11 leave 6	6 from 12 leave 6
4 from 11 leave 7	5 from 12 leave 7	6 from 13 leave 7
4 from 12 leave 8	5 from 13 leave 8	6 from 14 leave 8
4 from 13 leave 9	5 from 14 leave 9	6 from 15 leave 9

7 from 7 leave 0	8 from 8 leave 0	9 from 9 leave 0
7 from 8 leave 1	8 from 9 leave 1	9 from 10 leave 1
7 from 9 leave 2	8 from 10 leave 2	9 from 11 leave 2
7 from 10 leave 3	8 from 11 leave 3	9 from 12 leave 3
7 from 11 leave 4	8 from 12 leave 4	9 from 13 leave 4
7 from 12 leave 5	8 from 13 leave 5	9 from 14 leave 5
7 from 13 leave 6	8 from 14 leave 6	9 from 15 leave 6
7 from 14 leave 7	8 from 15 leave 7	9 from 16 leave 7
7 from 15 leave 8	8 from 16 leave 8	9 from 17 leave 8
7 from 16 leave 9	8 from 17 leave 9	9 from 18 leave 9

ORAL EXERCISES.

I.

What remains after taking :

6 from 7?	1 from 8?	1 from 9?	4 from 7?	5 from 5?
3 from 8?	1 from 1?	0 from 3?	2 from 2?	1 from 4?
0 from 1?	5 from 7?	2 from 6?	3 from 7?	3 from 8?
4 from 9?	4 from 5?	7 from 9?	1 from 6?	8 from 9?
1 from 2?	2 from 4?	8 from 8?	0 from 7?	2 from 7?
0 from 8?	2 from 8?	6 from 9?	7 from 8?	5 from 8?
7 from 7?	3 from 6?	1 from 7?	2 from 5?	3 from 4?
4 from 6?	1 from 5?	0 from 9?	3 from 5?	4 from 8?

II.

$15-7=?$	$15-8=?$	$17-8=?$	$18-8=?$	$15-3=?$
$10-8=?$	$11-2=?$	$14-7=?$	$13-9=?$	$12-9=?$
$12-3=?$	$17-9=?$	$11-6=?$	$12-8=?$	$11-1=?$
$13-6=?$	$13-5=?$	$10-2=?$	$14-2=?$	$18-3=?$
$10-9=?$	$10-6=?$	$16-7=?$	$16-6=?$	$11-3=?$
$14-6=?$	$12-5=?$	$14-8=?$	$14-3=?$	$18-7=?$
$12-7=?$	$16-9=?$	$12-8=?$	$17-6=?$	$14-4=?$
$13-4=?$	$11-8=?$	$18-5=?$	$16-2=?$	$13-2=?$

III.

Give remainders at sight :

		1st.	2d.	3d.	4th.	5th.	6th.	7th.	8th.
A.	{	12	11	14	10	16	14	18	11
		7	8	9	7	7	5	9	3
B.	{	10	11	13	12	10	18	14	13
		4	5	1	5	8	3	4	7
C.	{·	8	13	14	15	18	16	11	10
		0	8	1	4	4	1	1	5
D.	{	10	11	12	15	18	16	14	12
		6	9	6	8	7	4	8	2
E.	{	18	13	14	16	17	18	15	14
		6	9	2	3	9	5	2	0
F.	{	17	13	14	15	17	12	16	11
		6	2	6	9	5	3	5	3
G.	{	13	14	17	18	16	15	17	13
		5	7	0	8	6	3	3	6
H.	{	18	11	13	18	17	11	13	17
		2	4	3	1	8	2	0	2
I.	{	10	15	16	17	12	16	10	17
		1	7	9	1	9	8	9	4
J.	{	13	12	17	12	15	17	11	12
		4	4	7	8	1	6	6	1

IV.

$6+7-3=?$ | $14+4-9=?$ | $6-4+1=?$ | $10-(3+5)=?$
$8+4-5=?$ | $16+2-7=?$ | $16-3+7=?$ | $18-(7-2)=?$
$9+2-6=?$ | $13+3-1=?$ | $14-9+3=?$ | $9-(4+3)=?$
$7+7-5=?$ | $12+5-4=?$ | $9-8+6=?$ | $15-(6-1)=?$
$8+6-3=?$ | $15+0-8=?$ | $11-3+9=?$ | $13-(7+2)=?$
$9+8-6=?$ | $9+9-6=?$ | $7-4+6=?$ | $14-(5+4)=?$
$5+4-2=?$ | $16+1-7=?$ | $15-5+18=?$ | $16-?=9?$
$8+8-9=?$ | $11+3-5=?$ | $16-9+10=?$ | $10-?=6?$
$3+9-1=?$ | $10+4-8=?$ | $14-4+3=?$ | $13-?=7?$
$7+9-6=?$ | $12+4-9=?$ | $9-6+12=?$ | $18-?=11?$

V.

1. Subtract 5 from 6; 16; 26; 36; 46; 56; 66; 76.
2. Subtract 4 from 14; 44; 24; 94; 84; 64; 54; 34.
3. Subtract 7 from 13; 33; 23; 43; 14; 24; 64; 74.
4. Subtract 9 from 18; 28; 78; 97; 67; 15; 75; 85.
5. Subtract by threes from 29 to 2.   From 78 to 5.
6. Subtract by sixes from 45 to 3.   From 59 to 5.
7. Subtract by eights from 79 to 15.   From 98 to 2.
8. Subtract by twos from 63 to 1.   From 67 to 1.
9. Count by fives from 6 to 46 and back again.
10. Count by sevens from 9 to 72 and back again.
11. Subtract by nines from 100 to 1.   From 83 to 2.
12. Subtract by fours from 83 to 7.   From 79 to 3.
13. Subtract by fives from 60 to 0.   From 84 to 4.
14. Subtract by threes from 37.   From 41.   From 64.
15. Subtract by sevens from 53.   From 75.   From 86.
16. Subtract by sixes from 31.   From 90.   From 52.
17. Subtract by eights from 70.   From 43.   From 81.
18. Subtract by nines from 60.   From 50.   From 75.
19. Subtract by fours from 51.   From 63.   From 95.

VI.

1. Margaret bought 7 cakes, and eat 4. How many had she remaining ?

SOLUTION.—If Margaret bought 7 cakes and eat 4 of them, she must have remaining the difference between 7 cakes and 4 cakes, which is 3 cakes. Therefore, if Margaret bought 7 cakes and eat 4 of them, she has 3 cakes remaining.

2. George picked 6 quarts of strawberries, and William 4. How many more quarts did George pick than William ?

3. A boy had 9 cents, and spent 3 for fire-crackers. How many cents had he left ?

4. Albert caught 7 butterflies, but 2 got away. How many had he then ?

5. Jane bought 5 oranges, and gave away 2. How many had she for herself ?

6. Henry sold for 7 cents a kite that cost him 5 cents. How many cents did he gain ?

7. Charles rises at 6 o'clock, and studies till 8. How many hours does he employ in study ?

8. You have 8 fingers on both hands. Close 3 and tell me how many remain open.

9. If I borrow $12 and pay back $5, how much do I still owe ?

10. A boy had 16 rabbits, 7 of which were killed by a dog. How many rabbits has he left ?

11. Mr. Brown purchased $6 worth of provisions, and gave the clerk a $10 bill. How much change did he receive ?

12. In a class of 25 boys, 9 were detained for bad conduct. How many were dismissed ?

13. How many days from the 4th to the 27th of July ?

14. A boat containing 23 persons capsized, and 8 were drowned. How many were saved?

15. I bought a harness worth $22, and paid $5 on it. How much do I still owe?

16. In a company of soldiers there were 78 men. Of these 5 were killed, and 4 wounded. How many were fit for duty?

17. Abel is 8 years of age. How many years will pass before he is 55 years?

18. A school contained 9 more girls than boys. There were 67 girls. How many boys?

19. A farmer raised 38 tons of hay, and sold 6 of them. How many tons remain?

20. There were 16 persons in an omnibus. After 5 got out and 3 got in, how many persons were then in the "bus"?

21. In a ring there were 19 marbles. James shot away 6, and Edward 2. How many remained in the ring?

22. Richard had 27 marbles. He won 16 and lost 7. How many had he then?

23. William had 1 cent, and his uncle gave him 8 more. How much does he still want to purchase a pair of skates worth 79 cents?

24. There were 86 peaches on a tree. The wind blew off 5. How many peaches remained on the tree?

25. An arithmetic is worth 70 cents, and a slate is worth 8 cents. What is the difference of their prices?

26. Oliver had 15 lines to write from his history. He wrote 4 on Monday, and the same number on Tuesday. How many had he still to write?

27. James is 14 years old, Emma 4 years older, and Jessie 7 years younger than Emma. How old are Emma and Jessie?

28. James had 17 oranges. He gave 4 to Mary, 5 to Esther, and sold the rest. How many did he sell ?

29. 18 boys were going to have a swim ; 3 stopped to hear a hand organ, and 5 ran to a fire. How many went to swim ?

30. What is the difference between 16+11 and 2+8 ?

31. During a game of baseball one side made 9 runs, and the other 14. How many runs were made by one side more than the other ?

VII.

From 37 take 15.   From 52 take 48.

SOLUTION.—To subtract 15 from 37, we take the 5 units from the 7 units, and the one ten from the 3 tens, which leaves 2 tens and 2 units, or 22 units.

In the second example, we cannot take the 8 units from the 2 units; so we add to the 2 units 1 of the 5 tens, or 10 units, which makes 12 units. Then 8 units from 12 units leaves 4 units; and 4 tens from the 4 tens left in the minuend, leaves 0 tens. Hence, 48 from 52 leaves 4 units.

From 26 take 15.	From 87 take 36.	From 84 take 69.
From 47 take 21.	From 43 take 29.	From 56 take 27.
From 69 take 36.	From 62 take 47.	From 97 take 89.
From 74 take 23.	From 39 take 29.	From 42 take 26.
From 63 take 31.	From 28 take 19.	From 22 take 18.
From 15 take 11.	From 55 take 46.	From 31 take 29.
From 37 take 16.	From 37 take 35.	From 64 take 17.
From 99 take 63.	From 46 take 38.	From 91 take 36.
From 86 take 74.	From 73 take 66.	From 72 take 49.
From 28 take 21.	From 92 take 78.	From 88 take 67.
From 74 take 35.	From 54 take 48.	From 69 take 58.
From 27 take 19.	From 38 take 36.	From 90 take 26.
From 83 take 57.	From 70 take 16.	From 81 take 37.

VIII.

1. Martin had 25 cents, and spent 15 cents for a lunch. How many cents had he left?

2. From a flock of 87 sheep a farmer sold 26. How many had he remaining?

3. Purchased a watch for $47, and sold it for $34. How much did I lose?

4. Luke is 17 years old, and his father 58 years old. What is the difference of their ages?

5. A geography is worth 70 cents, and a small grammar 36 cents. How much more is the geography worth than the grammar?

6. In the last examination James had 75 per cent. and Henry 38 per cent. What per cent. had James more than Henry?

7. A person spent 37 cents in a store. What change did he receive if he gave a fifty-cent piece?

8. Joseph ran 84 rods, and William 56. How much farther did Joseph run than William?

9. The sum of two numbers is 75, and one of them is 25. What is the other?

10. A man sold a horse for $87, which was $18 more than it cost. What was the cost price?

11. John has 63 cents. If he spend 4 cents for marbles, 25 cents for a ball, and 5 cents for peanuts, how many cents will he have left?

12. A tree 58 feet high was broken off 46 feet from the top. How high is the remaining piece?

13. A foreman receives $80 a month. He pays $6 for a ton of coal, $20 for provisions, $3 for a pair of shoes, and $14 for sundry affairs. How much has he remaining?

14. A lady went shopping with one $5 bill and two

$10 bills. She spent $3 for ribbons, $6 for velvet, $7 for silk, and $2 for lining. How many dollars had she remaining?

15. A farmer having 64 sheep, sold 17 of them to A, 36 to B, and the remainder to C. How many did C receive?

16. 16 pupils were promoted from a class of 75; and on the same day 11 were received into the class. How many pupils were then in the class?

17. John had 26 cents, and his mother gave him 32. He then lost 17. How many cents had he left?

18. Sold a sled worth 87 cents for a penknife and 15 cents. What was the penknife worth?

19. Mr. White had $93 in bank. He took out $37 on Monday, and put in $26 the same afternoon. On Tuesday he took out $16 dollars. How much has he now in bank?

IX.

1. To 5 add 7; subtract 6; add 4; subtract 9; add 11; subtract 3; add 4; add 12; subtract 15; add 2. What is the result?

2. $7-2+5-1+9-6+12+1-5+20-37 = ?$

3. $6+17-11+37-6+2+5-25+7-30 = ?$

4. $18-12+4-10+1-1+6-3+7 = ?$

5. $3+7-4+5-1+10-6+2-8+1-3-6 = ?$

6. $3-2+9-8+6+4-2+10-6-8+4 = ?$

7. $17+8-6+10-8-3+7+4-6 = ?$

8. $47-7+10-25+5-6-4+3-13-7+4+2 = ?$

9. $38-1+3-30+17+3-16+2-7+1-4 = ?$

10. $67-8+1-50+47-6+7-8+32-2+8 = ?$

11. $46-26+17+7-8+3-16+2 = ?$

12. $18+7-5+32-6+7-2-8+16-7+23 = ?$

OPERATION OF SUBTRACTION.

1. What is the difference between 2153 and 5061 ?

OPERATION.

5061
2153
―――
2908

SOLUTION.—Place the less number under the greater, putting units under units, tens under tens, etc.

As 3 units cannot be taken from 1 unit, add 1 ten of the 6 tens of the minuend, or 10 units, to the 1 unit, making 11 units. 3 units from 11 units leave 8 units, which is written under units' column.

1 ten taken from the 6 tens of the minuend, leaves 5 tens; and 5 tens from 5 tens leave 0 tens.

1 hundred cannot be taken from 0 hundreds. Take 1 of the 5 thousands, or 10 hundreds, and from it subtract the 1 hundred of the subtrahend, putting the 9 hundreds thus found in hundreds' place in the remainder.

Lastly, 2 thousands from the 4 thousands left in the minuend, leave 2 thousands, which is written in thousands' place in the remainder.

NOTES.—1. In the beginning the pupil says: 3 from 11 leave 8; 5 from 5 leave 0; etc. But he should be gradually trained to name only results; thus, 8, 0, 9, 2.

2. The remainder, 0 tens, in the third paragraph above, may also be found by adding 1 to the 5 tens of the subtrahend, before subtracting. This operation is termed "carrying," while the former is called "borrowing." Both should be performed mentally.

PROOF.—Add the difference, or remainder, to the less number, and if the work be correct, we shall obtain the greater number.

ILLUSTRATIONS.

	2.	*3.*	*4.*	*5.*
From	378	720	198	$8650
Take	246	284	135	3725
	132	436	63	$4925
Proof	378	720	198	$8650

WRITTEN EXERCISES.

6. 895 — 371.	37. 6000 — 3006.	68. 456 — 390.
7. 178 — 153.	38. 493 — 387.	69. 2364 — 1008.
8. 387 — 152.	39. 4061 — 289.	70. 5307 — 48.
9. 396 — 312.	40. 537 — 29.	71. 4800 — 376.
10. 297 — 174.	41. 601 — 482.	72. 9854 — 7926.
11. 952 — 834.	42. 3971 — 896.	73. 44699 — 9886.
12. 733 — 214.	43. 4008 — 3196.	74. 67888 — 8096.
13. 487 — 329.	44. 2134 — 97.	75. 22003 — 10008.
14. 877 — 593.	45. 493 — 281.	76. 48909 — 19898.
15. 736 — 682.	46. 175 — 26.	77. 71968 — 50003.
16. 757 — 378.	47. 832 — 746.	78. 70000 — 69999.
17. 785 — 597.	48. 201 — 156.	79. 66901 — 8909.
18. 476 — 289.	49. 824 — 357.	80. 91111 — 8908.
19. 894 — 698.	50. 923 — 868.	81. 16843 — 13959.
20. 943 — 764.	51. 1002 — 491.	82. 57345 — 22198.
21. 587 — 364.	52. 796 — 485.	83. 35123 — 11207.
22. 829 — 74.	53. 371 — 296.	84. 82036 — 4804.
23. 700 — 309.	54. 4321 — 3924.	85. 21185 — 5706.
24. 186 — 98.	55. 862 — 674.	86. 58900 — 46304.
25. 200 — 45.	56. 502 — 209.	87. 353655 — 9447.
26. 9084 — 5579.	57. 738 — 21.	88. 478547 — 98215.
27. 6240 — 4089.	58. 892 — 406.	89. 847654 — 398007.
28. 5089 — 3009.	59. 56892 — 7964.	90. 504245 — 102907.
29. 9001 — 2532.	60. 5394 — 4096.	91. 642006 — 97719.
30. 7689 — 2147.	61. 792 — 485.	92. 703901 — 65809.
31. 7224 — 973.	62. 6931 — 5076.	93. 644305 — 509709.
32. 1096 — 982.	63. 392 — 289.	94. 458724 — 417384.
33. 4232 — 109.	64. 702 — 498.	95. 698447 — 525809.
34. 8624 — 4007.	65. 2020 — 1965.	96. 500702 — 309908.
35. 7586 — 397.	66. 70065 — 3962.	97. 201006 — 109207.
36. 3120 — 895.	67. 8434 — 7908.	98. 376210 — 265100.

99.	100.	101.	102.
465327	767070	218136	500190
9841	389106	37007	74275

103.	104.	105.	106.
800140	670506	130025	796111
37251	215330	62300	89003

107.	108.	109.	110.
666351	141012	750263	·571434
72009	84200	447864	89021

111.	112.	113.	114.
800000	500300	582399	304009
70096	18065	265174	170318

115.	116.	117.	118.
13500801	50001310	12030010	27008700
4070909	39010604	2100754	8910091

UNITED STATES CURRENCY.

21. To subtract *dollars* and *cents* write them as in addition, so that the separating points may fall in the same column.

1. From $92.06 subtract $43.27.

OPERATION.

$92.06, Minuend.

43.27, Subtrahend.

$48.79, Remainder.

SOLUTION.—Place the less number under the greater, taking care to have the points in the same column. Then proceed as in ordinary subtraction.

ILLUSTRATIONS.

	2.	*3.*	*4.*	*5.*
From	$43.25	$290.10	$330.00	$2060.50
Take	20.09	154.75	286.40	1800.75
	$23.16	$135.35	$43.60	$259.75

WRITTEN EXERCISES.

6.	*7.*	*8.*	*9.*
$590.15	$612.13	$915.50	$3210.90
201.00	482.25	850.75	1637.24

10.	*11.*	*12.*	*13.*
$3900.00	$1792.25	$4000.17	$1260.30
1585.20	1587.39	2050.25	942.00

14.	*15.*	*16.*	*17.*
$3705.00	$9185.74	$7000.75	$1000.72
816.73	2007.85	5309.87	652.80

18.	*19.*	*20.*	*21.*
$8156.12	$3780.37	$5111.31	$1500.60
3495.18	791.48	2886.32	725.63

22. A merchant bought flour for $679.50, and sold it for $982.25. What did he gain?

23. A and B together have $8270.66. If A has $4900.50, how much has B?

24. Having $75250.71 in the bank, I drew out $38700.80. How much have I remaining in the bank?

25. I bought a quantity of cloth for $780.78, and sold it for $1060.25. How much did I gain?

WRITTEN REVIEW.

1. A man sold his house for $5380, which was $670 more than it cost. What did it cost? *Ans.* $4710.

2. Mr. Brown and Mr. Smith together own $6790 worth of land. If Mr. Brown own $3960 worth, how much does Mr. Smith own? *Ans.* $2830.

3. How many years from the birth of Milton in 1608 to the birth of Washington in 1732? *Ans.* 124 years.

4. A gentleman borrowed $7983, and afterwards returned $3527. How much did he still owe?
Ans. $4456.

5. I bought 584 bushels of potatoes, and sold 96 bushels. How many bushels have I left?
Ans. 488 bushels.

6. General Zachary Taylor was born in 1790, and died in 1850. How old was he when he died?
Ans. 60 years.

7. The telescope was invented by Galileo in 1610. How many years since (1888) it was invented?
Ans. 278 years.

8. John earned $960 in a year, and William earned $175 less. How many dollars did William earn?
Ans. $785.

9. An architect received $65870 for building a house, and expended upon it $62965. What was his profit?
Ans. $2905.

10. Mr. Newton purchased a farm worth $15000, and paid on it $7900. How much remained due?
Ans. $7100.

11. A merchant commenced business with a capital of $45822, and retired with $90800. How much did he gain? *Ans.* $44978.

12. The sum of two numbers is 973, and the less is 284. What is the greater ?   *Ans.* 689.

13. In an army there were 27876 men, of whom 2009 were killed in battle. How many remained ?

Ans. 25867 men.

14. When General Garfield was elected President in 1880, he was 49 years old. In what year was he born ?

Ans. 1831.

15. One of two numbers is 983, and the other is 1206. What is their difference ?   *Ans.* 223.

16. A man purchased a cow for $27.50, and a span of horses for $179.75. How much did the horses cost more than the cow ?   *Ans.* $152.25.

17. A merchant sold for $3047 goods which cost him $976. How much did he gain by the transaction ?

Ans. $2071.

18. Thomas has 173 marbles less than Alexander, and Alexander has 300. How many has Thomas ?

Ans. 127 marbles.

19. America was discovered in 1492. How many years from that period to the Declaration of Independence in 1776 ?   *Ans.* 284 years.

20. What number is that which, taken from 1360, will leave 986 ?   *Ans.* 374.

21. The difference of two numbers is 987, and the greater is 19063. What is the less ?   *Ans.* 18076.

22. A farmer has 9083 sheep, and as many lambs lacking 587. How many lambs has he ?

Ans. 8496 lambs.

23. Joseph and Philip started from the same place, and travelled in the same direction. Joseph travelled 230 miles, and Philip 63. How far apart were they ?

Ans. 167 miles.

MULTIPLICATION.

22. *Multiplication* is the process of taking one number as many times as there are units in another.

NOTE.—Multiplication is a concise method of doing addition. Thus, to find how many books in 3 desks, each of which contains 4, instead of adding three 4's, we multiply 4 by 3, and obtain the same result.

MULTIPLICATION TABLE.

Once 0 is 0; twice 0 is 0; 0 taken any number of times is 0. 0 times 1 is 0; 0 times 2 is 0. 0 times any number is 0.

Once 1 is 1.	Twice 1 is 2.	3 times 1 is 3.
Once 2 are 2.	Twice 2 are 4.	3 times 2 are 6.
Once 3 are 3.	Twice 3 are 6.	3 times 3 are 9.
Once 4 are 4.	Twice 4 are 8.	3 times 4 are 12.
Once 5 are 5.	Twice 5 are 10.	3 times 5 are 15.
Once 6 are 6.	Twice 6 are 12.	3 times 6 are 18.
Once 7 are 7.	Twice 7 are 14.	3 times 7 are 21.
Once 8 are 8.	Twice 8 are 16.	3 times 8 are 24.
Once 9 are 9.	Twice 9 are 18.	3 times 9 are 27.
Once 10 are 10.	Twice 10 are 20.	3 times 10 are 30.
Once 11 are 11.	Twice 11 are 22.	3 times 11 are 33.
Once 12 are 12.	Twice 12 are 24.	3 times 12 are 36.

4 times 1 is 4.	4 times 5 are 20.	4 times 9 are 36.
4 times 2 are 8.	4 times 6 are 24.	4 times 10 are 40.
4 times 3 are 12.	4 times 7 are 28.	4 times 11 are 44.
4 times 4 are 16.	4 times 8 are 32.	4 times 12 are 48.

5 times 1 is 5.	5 times 5 are 25.	5 times 9 are 45.
5 times 2 are 10.	5 times 6 are 30.	5 times 10 are 50.
5 times 3 are 15.	5 times 7 are 35.	5 times 11 are 55.
5 times 4 are 20.	5 times 8 are 40.	5 times 12 are 60.

6 times 1 is 6.	6 times 5 are 30.	6 times 9 are 54.
6 times 2 are 12.	6 times 6 are 36.	6 times 10 are 60.
6 times 3 are 18.	6 times 7 are 42.	6 times 11 are 66.
6 times 4 are 24.	6 times 8 are 48.	6 times 12 are 72.

7 times 1 is 7.	8 times 1 is 8.	9 times 1 is 9.
7 times 2 are 14.	8 times 2 are 16.	9 times 2 are 18.
7 times 3 are 21.	8 times 3 are 24.	9 times 3 are 27.
7 times 4 are 28.	8 times 4 are 32.	9 times 4 are 36.
7 times 5 are 35.	8 times 5 are 40.	9 times 5 are 45.
7 times 6 are 42.	8 times 6 are 48.	9 times 6 are 54.
7 times 7 are 49.	8 times 7 are 56.	9 times 7 are 63.
7 times 8 are 56.	8 times 8 are 64.	9 times 8 are 72.
7 times 9 are 63.	8 times 9 are 72.	9 times 9 are 81.
7 times 10 are 70.	8 times 10 are 80.	9 times 10 are 90.
7 times 11 are 77.	8 times 11 are 88.	9 times 11 are 99.
7 times 12 are 84.	8 times 12 are 96.	9 times 12 are 108.

10 times 1 is 10.	11 times 1 is 11.	12 times 1 is 12.
10 times 2 are 20.	11 times 2 are 22.	12 times 2 are 24.
10 times 3 are 30.	11 times 3 are 33.	12 times 3 are 36.
10 times 4 are 40.	11 times 4 are 44.	12 times 4 are 48.
10 times 5 are 50.	11 times 5 are 55.	12 times 5 are 60.
10 times 6 are 60.	11 times 6 are 66.	12 times 6 are 72.
10 times 7 are 70.	11 times 7 are 77.	12 times 7 are 84.
10 times 8 are 80.	11 times 8 are 88.	12 times 8 are 96.
10 times 9 are 90.	11 times 9 are 99.	12 times 9 are 108.
10 times 10 are 100.	11 times 10 are 110.	12 times 10 are 120.
10 times 11 are 110.	11 times 11 are 121.	12 times 11 are 132.
10 times 12 are 120.	11 times 12 are 132.	12 times 12 are 144.

I.

How many are:

3 times 9 ?	2 times 9 ?	3 times 2 ?	2 times 5 ?
2 times 7 ?	7 times 4 ?	2 times 6 ?	9 times 1 ?
5 times 6 ?	9 times 6 ?	8 times 3 ?	7 times 8 ?
6 times 8 ?	8 times 8 ?	3 times 6 ?	4 times 5 ?
9 times 9 ?	5 times 1 ?	5 times 5 ?	7 times 1 ?
2 times 1 ?	2 times 4 ?	6 times 4 ?	6 times 6 ?
9 times 7 ?	4 times 9 ?	5 times 3 ?	7 times 3 ?
8 times 5 ?	6 times 7 ?	7 times 7 ?	9 times 5 ?
2 times 2 ?	3 times 3 ?	4 times 8 ?	8 times 9 ?
3 times 4 ?	7 times 5 ?	8 times 2 ?	4 times 4 ?

II.

Multiply 13 by 5.

SOLUTION.—5 times 3 units are 15 units, or 1 ten and 5 units. 5 times 1 ten is 5 tens, which, with the 1 ten found in multiplying the units, make 6 tens. Hence, 5 times 13 units are 6 tens and 5 units, or 65 units.

$13 \times 4 = ?$	$16 \times 5 = ?$	$11 \times 10 = ?$	$18 \times 2 = ?$
$15 \times 2 = ?$	$12 \times 11 = ?$	$10 \times 10 = ?$	$11 \times 7 = ?$
$12 \times 7 = ?$	$18 \times 6 = ?$	$18 \times 9 = ?$	$16 \times 7 = ?$
$14 \times 3 = ?$	$17 \times 3 = ?$	$14 \times 7 = ?$	$14 \times 5 = ?$
$11 \times 11 = ?$	$14 \times 8 = ?$	$17 \times 8 = ?$	$12 \times 6 = ?$
$10 \times 4 = ?$	$12 \times 10 = ?$	$15 \times 4 = ?$	$17 \times 9 = ?$
$15 \times 6 = ?$	$15 \times 9 = ?$	$12 \times 12 = ?$	$10 \times 2 = ?$
$17 \times 5 = ?$	$18 \times 4 = ?$	$13 \times 6 = ?$	$15 \times 8 = ?$
$12 \times 9 = ?$	$16 \times 8 = ?$	$16 \times 3 = ?$	$13 \times 5 = ?$
$13 \times 7 = ?$	$13 \times 9 = ?$	$14 \times 2 = ?$	$18 \times 7 = ?$
$12 \times 6 = ?$	$14 \times 2 = ?$	$15 \times 4 = ?$	$12 \times 9 = ?$
$10 \times 9 = ?$	$16 \times 3 = ?$	$17 \times 3 = ?$	$18 \times 1 = ?$
$15 \times 3 = ?$	$14 \times 5 = ?$	$16 \times 6 = ?$	$13 \times 6 = ?$

III.

NOTE.—Only a part of the following exercises should be written on the blackboard at one lesson.   When the answers can be readily given from below, they should be required from above.

Give results at sight :

A. {	4	1	3	6	5	9	8	7	2
	5	2	9	8	7	4	2	3	6
B. {	1	4	6	2	5	1	5	9	4
	9	7	5	4	2	3	5	2	8
C. {	2	4	2	4	3	5	4	1	9
	7	1	2	3	8	9	4	5	9
D. {	3	7	8	6	2	3	6	5	6
	3	9	8	7	3	5	4	8	9
E. {	6	1	3	8	7	8	6	7	8
	6	7	6	1	8	9	1	7	5
F. {	2	13	4	11	4	15	14	11	12
	17	3	10	5	16	2	7	11	10
G. {	16	3	15	6	2	11	13	2	16
	9	17	4	12	13	14	10	14	3
H. {	11	16	7	14	11	7	12	10	17
	13	2	15	6	3	10	4	11	12
I. {	12	3	13	6	9	12	8	13	10
	12	15	4	11	10	2	11	12	15

J. $\{$	17	15	5	13	4	10	11	16	12
	11	12	16	7	11	6	12	6	16

K. $\{$	10	5	14	9	10	3	14	7	16
	10	15	9	11	8	10	4	17	7

L. $\{$	10	8	15	7	10	9	15	8	9
	12	16	9	11	5	17	8	13	12

M. $\{$	11	17	2	3	13	5	14	11	10
	16	8	10	12	5	17	12	15	11

N. $\{$	16	10	6	15	7	13	5	17	12
	12	17	17	6	12	6	14	4	8

O. $\{$	10	16	3	13	11	14	18	12	19
	14	10	14	9	2	8	12	5	11

IV.

$6 \times 9 + 2 = ?$	$8 \times 9 + 24 = ?$	$(6+7) \times 3 = ?$
$8 \times 7 + 9 = ?$	$16 \times 5 - 18 = ?$	$(14-3) \times 6 = ?$
$7 \times 9 + 17 = ?$	$14 \times 6 + 60 = ?$	$(16-4) \times 9 = ?$
$12 \times 11 + 8 = ?$	$9 \times 5 - 15 = ?$	$(11-6) \times 7 = ?$
$15 \times 6 + 9 = ?$	$17 \times 4 - 15 = ?$	$(20-2) \times 5 = ?$
$8 \times 6 - 4 = ?$	$15 \times 6 + 10 = ?$	$(13 \times 1) \times 4 = ?$
$12 \times 9 - 18 = ?$	$18 \times 8 - 51 = ?$	$(6+2) \times 11 = ?$
$7 \times 6 - 2 = ?$	$8 \times 4 - 30 = ?$	$(1+9) \times 5 = ?$
$13 \times 8 - 12 = ?$	$7 \times 12 + 3 = ?$	$(28-15) \times 2 = ?$
$11 \times 11 - 11 = ?$	$7 \times 7 + 11 = ?$	$(21-6) + 5 = ?$
$30 - 6 \times 4 = ?$	$62 - 12 \times 4 = ?$	$28 - 16 \times 4 = ?$
$19 + 11 \times 11 = ?$	$28 + 6 \times 16 = ?$	$13 + 13 \times 4 = ?$
$37 - 19 \times 4 = ?$	$31 + 9 \times 8 = ?$	$69 - 17 + 5 = ?$

V.

Multiply 21 by 9 ; 31 by 8 ; 41 by 7 ; 5 by 6 ; 61 by 5 ; 72 by 4 ; 82 by 3 ; 92 by 3.

Multiply 83 by 2 ; 73 by 3 ; 22 by 8 ; 32 by 7 ; 60 by 4 ; 53 by 5 ; 43 by 6 ; 94 by 9.

Multiply 65 by 3 ; 34 by 6 ; 20 by 7 ; 44 by 5 ; 75 by 2 ; 54 by 4 ; 84 by 9 ; 90 by 8.

Multiply 56 by 3 ; 25 by 6 ; 36 by 5 ; 66 by 2 ; 87 by 8 ; 40 by 4 ; 76 by 9 ; 97 by 7.

Multiply 37 by 4 ; 58 by 2 ; 47 by 3 ; 98 by 6 ; 89 by 7 ; 27 by 5 ; 68 by 9 ; 99 by 8.

VI.

1. What will 3 pounds of raisins cost at 11 cents a pound ?

SOLUTION.—If 1 pound of raisins cost 11 cents, 3 pounds will cost 3 times as much as 1 pound, or 3 times 11 cents, which are 33 cents. Therefore, if 1 pound of raisins cost 11 cents, 3 pounds will cost 33 cents.

2. What cost 2 spools of thread at 5 cents apiece?

3. In one gallon there are four quarts. How many quarts in 7 gallons ? 9 gallons ? 20 gallons ?

4. There are 7 days in a week. How many days in 9 weeks ? 5 weeks ? 3 weeks ? 13 weeks ? 15 weeks ?

5. What will 6 pounds of cheese cost at 9 cents a pound ?

6. If you solve 8 problems a day, how many will you solve in 5 days ? 7 days? 3 days ? 2 days ?

7. At 12 cents apiece what will 8 primers cost ?

8. James earns $6 a week, and Henry $3. How much will both earn in 3 weeks ? 9 weeks ? 13 weeks ?

9. How many inches in 9 feet, each foot containing

10. What will 13 tons of coal cost at $7 a ton ? At $6 ? At $8 ? At $5 ?

11. John bought 6 rubber balls at 16 cents each. How much change should he receive from a dollar ?

12. A man travelled by stage at the rate of 8 miles an hour. How far did he travel in 9 hours? 11 hours? 16 hours ? 18 hours ?

13. I bought 3 pounds of beef at 18 cents a pound, and 11 pounds of rice at 11 cents a pound. What did both cost ?

14. What will be the cost of 7 pounds of coffee at 17 cents a pound, and 1 pound of tea at 75 cents a pound ?

15. Two persons travel in the same direction, one 38 miles a day, and the other 24. How far apart are they at the end of 6 days ? 2 days ? 9 days ?

16. A tailor bought 15 yards of cloth at $5 a yard ; but being damaged, he was obliged to sell it at a loss of $13. How much did he receive for it ?

17. Joseph has 11 chestnuts, and Henry 3 times as many less 16. How many has Henry ?

18. Two men start from the same point, and travel in opposite directions, one 34 miles a day, and the other 26. How far apart are they in 5 days ?

19. How many handkerchiefs in 8 boxes, each containing 25 of them ?

20. Two men travelled toward each other, one 4 miles an hour, and the other 3. They had been travelling 22 hours before they met. How far apart were they ?

21. What cost 4 base-balls at 75 cents apiece ?

22. A boy earned 67 cents a day, and paid 47 cents of it for board. How much had he at the end of 6 days?

23. Bought 9 loads of wheat at $30 a load, and sold it for $300. How much did I gain ?

24. What cost 2 pairs of gloves at 67 cents a pair ?

25. A carpenter earned $18 a week, and a shoemaker $11. How much more than the shoemaker will the carpenter have earned in 16 weeks ?

26. If a man dig 27 bushels of potatoes in one day, how many will he dig in 6 days ? 7 days ? 3 days ?

27. What is the amount of the following bill : 6 quarts of soft soap at 11 cents a quart ; 7 cakes of soap at 9 cents each ; and 2 brooms at 35 cents apiece ?

28. If 7 men do a piece of work in 19 days, how long will it take one man to do it ?

29. How many pounds of coffee in 4 bags, each containing 46 pounds ? 37 pounds ? 50 pounds ?

30. If 12 men build a wall in 12 days, how long will it take one man to build it ?

31. There are 16 ounces in 1 pound. How many ounces in 5 pounds ? 9 pounds ? 3 pounds ? 2 pounds ?

32. If 5 yards be required to make one suit of clothes, how many yards will 5 suits require ? 3 suits ? 7 suits ?

33. If a pound of butter cost 23 cents, what will 9 pounds cost ?

34. A farmer sold 16 bushels of potatoes to one man, 20 to another, and 32 to a third, at $2 per bushel. How much did he receive ?

35. William is 15 years old, and his Uncle Charles is 4 times as old. What is the sum of their ages ?

36. A farmer exchanged 17 barrels of apples, worth $5 a barrel, for 12 cords of wood at $7 a cord. Did he gain or lose, and how much ?

37. If peaches are worth 3 cents apiece, how much will 20 cost ? 15 ? 30 ? 40 ?

38. Find the cost of 12 yards of ribbon at 4 cents a yard, and 16 spools of thread at 5 cents a spool.

VII.

1. $6 \times 4, -3, +9, \times 2, -40, +5, \times 4 = ?$
2. $18 - 8, \times 10, -75, \times 2, -50, +1 = ?$
3. $37 + 3, -30, \times 6, +17, -65, \times 8 = ?$
4. $14 \times 4, -6, +13, +17, -65, \times 2, \times 11, -30 = ?$
5. $12 \times 9, -90, \times 3, -4, +11, -37, \times 5, -16 = ?$
6. $130 - 75, +5, \times 8, -400, +20, -68, \times 3 = ?$
7. $7 + 3, -4, +27, -6, -12, \times 8, -26 = ?$
8. $144 - 24, +80, -170, \times 2, +4, -30, \times 2, -64 = ?$
9. $19 + 7, \times 5, -125, +9, -3, \times 12, -32, -16 = ?$
10. $33 - 13, \times 8, -70, +10, \times 3, -150, +25 = ?$
11. $60 + 5, -25, \times 2, +10, -50, -15 = ?$
12. $30 \times 3, -60, +5, \times 2, -40, +20, \times 2 = ?$

WRITTEN EXERCISES.

1. Multiply 6370 by 6.

OPERATION.

6370
6
——
38220

SOLUTION.—6 times 0 units is 0 units. 6 times 7 tens are 42 tens, or 4 hundreds and 2 tens. The 2 tens are written in tens' place, and the 4 hundreds are kept to be added to the hundreds.

6 times 3 hundreds are 18 hundreds, which, with the 4 hundreds reserved, make 22 hundreds, or 2 thousands and 2 hundreds. The 2 hundreds are put in hundreds' place, and the 2 thousands reserved to be added to the thousands.

6 times 6 thousands are 36 thousands, which, with the 2 thousands reserved, make 38 thousands. Hence, 6 times 6370 are 38220.

ILLUSTRATIONS.

2.	*3.*	*4.*	*5.*	*6.*	*7.*
213	432	341	526	\$7.43	\$5.26
1	3	4	6	7	5
213	1296	1364	3156	\$52.01	\$26.30

Multiply :

8. 879 by 7.	*19.* 856 by 9.	*30.* 378 by 7.
9. 692 by 6.	*20.* 763 by 8.	*31.* 267 by 9.
10. 796 by 8.	*21.* 259 by 7.	*32.* 156 by 5.
11. 476 by 3.	*22.* 387 by 6.	*33.* 801 by 2.
12. 582 by 5.	*23.* 954 by 9.	*34.* 307 by 4.
13. 607 by 6.	*24.* 832 by 4.	*35.* 471 by 6.
14. 840 by 3.	*25.* 604 by 8.	*36.* 167 by 9.
15. 736 by 2.	*26.* 386 by 4.	*37.* 516 by 7.
16. 913 by 4.	*27.* 945 by 7.	*38.* 165 by 2.
17. 619 by 6.	*28.* 776 by 6.	*39.* 722 by 8.
18. 495 by 3.	*29.* 525 by 8.	*40.* 249 by 4.

41. 3807 by 9.	*57.* 783206 by 7.	*73.* 5820009 by 5.
42. 2918 by 7.	*58.* 405182 by 6.	*74.* 2000199 by 8.
43. 4792 by 8.	*59.* 178420 by 5.	*75.* 88960010 by 5.
44. 7587 by 4.	*60.* 473824 by 5.	*76.* 58629112 hy 9.
45. 6315 by 6.	*61.* 218793 by 9.	*77.* 16509031 by 7.
46. 9054 by 5.	*62.* 380697 by 2.	*78.* 20506030 by 9.
47. 8117 by 2.	*63.* 307901 by 8.	*79.* 44889100 by 4.
48. 3948 by 3.	*64.* 904905 by 3.	*80.* 333666111 by 3.
49. 79458 by 8.	*65.* 302163 by 7.	*81.* 565656222 by 4.
50. 27935 by 7.	*66.* 235619 by 6.	*82.* 989000625 by 2.
51. 17092 by 9.	*67.* 819273 by 5.	*83.* 505404101 by 6.
52. 46181 by 4.	*68.* 193111 by 4.	*84.* 777888222 by 3.
53. 31953 by 5.	*69.* 374952 by 8.	*85.* 800300701 by 5.
54. 67209 by 8.	*70.* 506044 by 9.	*86.* 900430230 by 6.
55. 36431 by 9.	*71.* 1547006 by 4.	*87.* 755313200 by 7.
56. 90038 by 6.	*72.* 3900740 by 8.	*88.* 112312612 by 8.

89. 400002571 by 9.	*92.* 673501211 by 9.
90. 492563128 by 7.	*93.* 240514630 by 6.
91. 303773827 by 8.	*94.* 800200709 by 8.

95. 768456781 by 9. | *98.* 998863789 by 7.
96. 582974327 by 5. | *99.* 654879396 by 8.
97. 675329877 by 6. | *100.* 877695869 by 9.

WRITTEN EXERCISES.

1. Multiply 732 by 47.

OPERATION.

```
  732
   47
 ────
 5124 = 732 ×  7
 2928 = 732 × 40
 ─────
34404 = 732 × 47
```

SOLUTION.—Put 47 under 732 so that units shall stand under units, tens under tens, etc.

First multiply by the 7 units; and then by the 4 tens, placing the right-hand figure of the tens' product under the tens of the units' product. Add the two results, and the sum will be the answer required.

ILLUSTRATIONS.

2.	*3.*	*4.*	*5.*
327	46	316	435
46	327	63	78
1962	• 322	948	3480
1308	92	1896	3045
15042	138	19908	33930
	15042		

6.	*7.*	*8.*	*9.*	*10.*
263	425	548	318	862
32	21	45	25	59

11. 322 by 37. *Ans.* 11914.
12. 219 by 24.   *Ans.* 5256.
13. 631 by 23. *Ans.* 14513.
14. 533 by 42. *Ans.* 22386.
15. 211 by 51. *Ans.* 10761.

16. 308 by 34. *Ans.* 10472.
17. 412 by 61. *Ans.* 25132.
18. 271 by 43. *Ans.* 11653.
19. 404 by 22.   *Ans.* 8888.
20. 302 by 45. *Ans.* 13590.

21. 521 by 39. *Ans.* 20319. | *36.* 839 by 89. *Ans.* 74671.
22. 644 by 76. *Ans.* 48944. | *37.* 319 by 75. *Ans.* 23925.
23. 978 by 41. *Ans.* 40098. | *38.* 417 by 93. *Ans.* 38781.
24. 872 by 47. *Ans.* 40984. | *39.* 523 by 87. *Ans.* 45501.
25. 761 by 58. *Ans.* 44138. | *40.* 198 by 76. *Ans.* 15048.
26. 408 by 69. *Ans.* 28152. | *41.* 879 by 34. *Ans.* 29886.
27. 607 by 78. *Ans.* 47346. | *42.* 725 by 77. *Ans.* 55825.
28. 329 by 84. *Ans.* 27636. | *43.* 306 by 37. *Ans.* 11322.
29. 534 by 93. *Ans.* 49662. | *44.* 696 by 58. *Ans.* 40368.
30. 285 by 74. *Ans.* 21090. | *45.* 287 by 69. *Ans.* 19803.
31. 862 by 49. *Ans.* 42238. | *46.* 914 by 28. *Ans.* 25592.
32. 794 by 24. *Ans.* 19056. | *47.* 549 by 68. *Ans.* 37332.
33. 827 by 52. *Ans.* 43004. | *48.* 705 by 99. *Ans.* 69795.
34. 502 by 71. *Ans.* 35642. | *49.* 367 by 52. *Ans.* 19084.
35. 288 by 42. *Ans.* 12096. | *50.* 497 by 44. *Ans.* 21868.

51. 3447 by 63. *Ans.* 217161. | *68.* 5630 by 404.
52. 2316 by 18. *Ans.* 41688. | *69.* 52877 by 128.
53. 8736 by 96. *Ans.* 838656. | *70.* 18624 by 233.
54. 5485 by 88. *Ans.* 482680. | *71.* 70391 by 486.
55. 7137 by 25. *Ans.* 178425. | *72.* 65197 by 175.
56. 8409 by 63. *Ans.* 529767. | *73.* 72394 by 271.
57. 6523 by 35. *Ans.* 228305. | *74.* 93164 by 315.
58. 9046 by 47. *Ans.* 425162. | *75.* 41282 by 436.
59. 7316 by 235. *Ans.* 1719260.| *76.* 54739 by 316.
60. 6893 by 123. *Ans.* 847839. | *77.* 85321 by 427.
61. 4503 by 207. *Ans.* 932121. | *78.* 43246 by 245.
62. 7096 by 235. *Ans.* 1667560.| *79.* 74871 by 562.
63. 8967 by 907. *Ans.* 8133069.| *80.* 36547 by 374.
64. 4963 by 294. *Ans.* 1459122.| *81.* 26293 by 853.
65. 8963 by 204. *Ans.* 1828452.| *82.* 89785 by 976.
66. 7006 by 752. *Ans.* 5268512.| *83.* 75482 by 735.
67. 4006 by 305. *Ans.* 1221830.| *84.* 68673 by 193.

85. 907284 by 352.
86. 730725 by 639.
87. 2842753 by 784.
88. 9316924 by 628.
89. 9454765 by 475.
90. 975784899 by 802.
91. 684752907 by 743.
92. 897564689 by 345.
93. 984794847 by 456.
94. 658874854 by 518.
95. 796008453 by 673.
96. 674657437 by 769.
97. 998547364 by 892.
98. 678836955 by 678.
99. 784344698 by 586.
100. 489694957 by 705.
101. 875508607 by 678.
102. 796467384 by 769.
103. 508706229 by 896.
104. 98365725 by 2096.
105. 39560734 by 3984.
106. 78562916 by 5863.
107. 45300779 by 8097.
108. 88966781 by 6357.

109. 507325 by 786464.
110. 896325 by 817595.
111. 963005 by 187684.
112. 802967 by 256632.
113. 885403 by 800719.
114. 760597 by 321828.
115. 950324 by 548237.
116. 608532976 by 3005.
117. 872231675 by 4731.
118. 275894115 by 8763.
119. 388765444 by 5009.
120. 675421366 by 2824.
121. 841222598 by 1253.
122. 784232 by 74563.
123. 134085 by 29386.
124. 674207 by 30075.
125. 5000307 by 40904.
126. 7500008 by 50006.
127. 39085007 by 12009.
128. 300400902 by 80703.
129. 81500327 by 80007.
130. 7430509 by 13008.
131. 2470802 by 73009.
132. 89047983 by 589476.

CONTRACTIONS.

23. To multiply a number by 10, annex one cipher ; to multiply it by 100, annex two ciphers ; to multiply it by 1000, annex three ciphers ; and so on.

When there are ciphers at the right of one or both of the numbers to be multiplied, omit them in multiplying, and annex as many to the result.

ILLUSTRATIONS.

1. Multiply 74 by 320. | *2.* Multiply 6900 by 480.

OPERATION.

```
      74
      32|0
     ----
     148
     222
     -----
   23680
```

OPERATION.

```
    69|00
    48|0
    ----
    552
    276
    -------
  3312000
```

WRITTEN EXERCISES.

Multiply :

3. 567 by 10. | *12.* 1872 by 130. | *21.* 4280 by 300.
4. 986 by 100. | *13.* 7561 by 120. | *22.* 71200 by 400.
5. 359 by 100. | *14.* 8065 by 470. | *23.* 64000 by 500.
6. 875 by 300. | *15.* 6294 by 240. | *24.* 86000 by 340.
7. 937 by 200. | *16.* 8731 by 360. | *25.* 76000 by 180.
8. 763 by 100. | *17.* 1230 by 180. | *26.* 44010 by 2000.
9. 825 by 400. | *18.* 6810 by 150. | *27.* 85500 by 1500.
10. 532 by 500. | *19.* 9037 by 170. | *28.* 64000 by 6100.
11. 879 by 600. | *20.* 1419 by 140. | *29.* 47050 by 3000.

30. 52000 by 10600. | *34.* 650000 by 603000.
31. 10900 by 158000. | *35.* 108000 by 490000.
32. 36000 by 207000. | *36.* 291600 by 500000.
33. 891200 by 900000. | *37.* 730000 by 702000.

UNITED STATES CURRENCY.

24. When one of the factors contain *cents*, or *dollars* and *cents*, multiply as in simple numbers. Point off two places from the right, in the product, and prefix the sign $.

1. What cost 27 tons of coal at $5.75 a ton ?

OPERATION.

$5.75
27
—————
4025
1150
—————
$155.25

SOLUTION.—If one ton cost $5.75, 27 tons will cost 27 times $5.75, which is $155.25. Since the multiplicand contains cents, we must point off two places in the product.

WRITTEN EXERCISES.

2. What will 37 barrels of flour cost at $6.85 a barrel ?
Ans. $253.45.

3. Multiply $472.66 by 27. *Ans.* $12761.82.

4. Multiply $1826.37 by 160. *Ans.* $292219.20.

5. Multiply $892.06 by 327. *Ans.* $291703.62.

6. Multiply $2932.25 by 1408. *Ans.* $4128608.00.

7. If an acre of land is worth $237.82, what are 482 acres worth ? *Ans.* $114629.24.

8. At $4.80 a bushel, what will 625 bushels of flaxseed cost ? *Ans.* $3000.00.

9. What cost 83 bushels of corn, at 75 cents a bushel ?
Ans. $62.25.

10. What cost 145 yards of sheeting at 8 cents a yard ?
Ans. $11.60.

11. At $4.63 a head, what will 378 sheep cost ?
Ans. $1750.14.

12. What cost 8 pieces of calico, each piece containing 25 yards, at 7 cents a yard ? *Ans.* $14.00.

13. How much will a grocer pay for 2 chests of tea, each containing 65 pounds, at 65 cents a pound ?
Ans. $84.50.

14. What will 19 hogsheads of vinegar cost, each containing 63 gallons, at 23 cents a gallon ? *Ans.* $275.31.

15. Bought 9 cows at $30 each, 13 horses at $135 each, and 300 sheep at $3.50 each. What was the entire cost?   *Ans.* $3075.

16. A merchant purchased 27 pieces of cloth, each containing 54 yards, at $3.33 a yard, and sold it for $3.45 a yard. How much did he gain?   *Ans.* $174.96.

17. A flour merchant bought 450 barrels of flour for $3262.50, and sold it for $8.63 a barrel. What did he gain?   *Ans.* $621.00.

18. A man earns $3.25 a day, and his daily expenses are $1.89. How much will he save in 365 days?
                                            Ans. $496.40.

19. I sold 13 bales of cotton cloth, each bale containing 10 pieces, and each piece 19 yards, at 5 cents per yard. What did I receive for the whole?

WRITTEN REVIEW.

1. If a man save $325 in one year, what will he save in 15 years?

SOLUTION.—If a man save $325 in one year, in 15 years he will save 15 times as much as in one year, or 15 times $325, which is $4875.

2. What will be the cost of 56 miles of railroad at $15760 a mile?   *Ans.* $882560.

3. A grocer bought 12 tubs of butter, each containing 45 pounds, at 30 cents a pound, and 23 tubs of another kind, each containing 56 pounds, at 35 cents a pound. What was the cost of the whole?   *Ans.* $612.80.

4. If it take 345 stitches to hem one side of a pocket-handkerchief, how many stitches would it take to hem 9 handkerchiefs?   *Ans.* 6210.

5. How long will it take 1 man to do a piece of work, if 5 men can do it in 30 days ? *Ans.* 150 days.

6. How much hay would be required to feed 50 horses for 14 weeks, if one horse eat 196 pounds in one week ? *Ans.* 137200 pounds.

7. If 8 quarts make a peck, and 4 pecks make a bushel, how many quarts in 980 bushels ? *Ans.* 31360 quarts.

8. In a block of houses there are 56 buildings, each building containing 45 windows, and each window 16 panes of glass. How many panes of glass in the whole block of buildings ? *Ans.* 40320 panes.

9. If it require 213 tons of iron worth $75 a ton to build one mile of a railroad, what will be the cost of iron enough to build a railroad 365 miles long ? *Ans.* $5830875.

10. What will a carpenter pay for 36 boards, each 16 feet long, at 8 cents a foot ? *Ans.* $46.08.

11. If Mr. Noah can set 1200 ems of type in an hour, how many ems can he set in 58 days of 9 hours each ? *Ans.* 626400 ems.

12. What amount of money will enable me to give $84 to each of 354 laborers ? *Ans.* $29736.

13. In a book of 475 pages, the words average 8 letters to a word, and 9 words to a line. If there are on an average 38 lines to a page, how many letters in the book ? *Ans.* 1299600 letters.

14. When the market price of beef is 18 cents a pound, what will 631 pounds cost ? *Ans.* $113.58.

15. What will Mr. Owen pay for a farm of 579 acres, at $64 an acre ? *Ans.* $37056.

16. Bought 63 cases of French calf boots, each case containing 15 pairs. What was the cost at $5.50 a pair ? *Ans.* $5197.50.

17. A merchant shipped 230 barrels of flour at $8.50 a barrel, and the same quantity of apples at $3.50 a barrel. What was the value of both ?   *Ans.* $2760.

18. What will 63 gallons of wine cost, at the rate of $3.75 a gallon ?   *Ans.* $236.25.

19. How far will a boy skate in 5 days, if he skate 6 hours a day, at the rate of 6 miles an hour ?
Ans. 180 miles.

20. How many pounds of tea in 1625 chests, each chest containing 68 pounds ?   *Ans.* 110500 pounds.

21. Sold 23 bales of cloth, each containing 82 yards, at 65 cents a yard. How much did I receive for it ?
Ans. $1225.90.

22. Purchased 945 tons of hay at $25 a ton. How much did it cost?   *Ans.* $23625.

23. What will 1860 barrels of flour cost at $4.35 per barrel ?   *Ans.* $8091.

24. At 37 bushels per acre, how many bushels of wheat will 650 acres produce?   *Ans.* 24050 bushels.

25. If one plantation of 90 acres is worth $27 per acre, and another of 105 acres is worth $19 per acre, what is the value of both plantations?   *Ans.* $4425.

26. How many pages in 4820 books, if each book contains 242 pages ?   *Ans.* 1166440 pages.

27. I bought 36 barrels of pork at $18 a barrel, and sold it for $820. How much did I gain ?   *Ans.* $172.

28. If one train runs 28 miles an hour for 24 hours, how many miles, more or less, will another train run in 22 hours at 32 miles per hour ?   *Ans.* 32 miles more.

29. A carpenter employed on a building for 96 days, received $3.75 a day. His expenses were $1.65 a day. How much did he save ?   *Ans.* $201.60.

DIVISION.

25. *Division* is the process of finding how many times one number is contained in another of the same kind.

DIVISION TABLE.

0 divided by 1 equals 0; 0 divided by 2 equals 0; 0 divided by any number equals 0.

$1 \div 1 = 1.$	$2 \div 2 = 1.$	$3 \div 3 = 1.$	$4 \div 4 = 1.$
$2 \div 1 = 2.$	$4 \div 2 = 2.$	$6 \div 3 = 2.$	$8 \div 4 = 2.$
$3 \div 1 = 3.$	$6 \div 2 = 3.$	$9 \div 3 = 3.$	$12 \div 4 = 3.$
$4 \div 1 = 4.$	$8 \div 2 = 4.$	$12 \div 3 = 4.$	$16 \div 4 = 4.$
$5 \div 1 = 5.$	$10 \div 2 = 5.$	$15 \div 3 = 5.$	$20 \div 4 = 5.$
$6 \div 1 = 6.$	$12 \div 2 = 6.$	$18 \div 3 = 6.$	$24 \div 4 = 6.$
$7 \div 1 = 7.$	$14 \div 2 = 7.$	$21 \div 3 = 7.$	$28 \div 4 = 7.$
$8 \div 1 = 8.$	$16 \div 2 = 8.$	$24 \div 3 = 8.$	$32 \div 4 = 8.$
$9 \div 1 = 9.$	$18 \div 2 = 9.$	$27 \div 3 = 9.$	$36 \div 4 = 9.$
$5 \div 5 = 1.$	$6 \div 6 = 1.$	$7 \div 7 = 1.$	$8 \div 8 = 1.$
$10 \div 5 = 2.$	$12 \div 6 = 2.$	$14 \div 7 = 2.$	$16 \div 8 = 2.$
$15 \div 5 = 3.$	$18 \div 6 = 3.$	$21 \div 7 = 3.$	$24 \div 8 = 3.$
$20 \div 5 = 4.$	$24 \div 6 = 4.$	$28 \div 7 = 4.$	$32 \div 8 = 4.$
$25 \div 5 = 5.$	$30 \div 6 = 5.$	$35 \div 7 = 5.$	$40 \div 8 = 5.$
$30 \div 5 = 6.$	$36 \div 6 = 6.$	$42 \div 7 = 6.$	$48 \div 8 = 6.$
$35 \div 5 = 7.$	$42 \div 6 = 7.$	$49 \div 7 = 7.$	$56 \div 8 = 7.$
$40 \div 5 = 8.$	$48 \div 6 = 8.$	$56 \div 7 = 8.$	$64 \div 8 = 8.$
$45 \div 5 = 9,$	$54 \div 6 = 9,$	$63 \div 7 = 9,$	$72 \div 8 = 9,$

$9 \div 9 = 1.$	$10 \div 10 = 1.$	$11 \div 11 = 1.$	$12 \div 12 = 1.$
$18 \div 9 = 2.$	$20 \div 10 = 2.$	$22 \div 11 = 2.$	$24 \div 12 = 2.$
$27 \div 9 = 3.$	$30 \div 10 = 3.$	$33 \div 11 = 3.$	$36 \div 12 = 3.$
$36 \div 9 = 4.$	$40 \div 10 = 4.$	$44 \div 11 = 4.$	$48 \div 12 = 4.$
$45 \div 9 = 5.$	$50 \div 10 = 5.$	$55 \div 11 = 5.$	$60 \div 12 = 5.$
$54 \div 9 = 6.$	$60 \div 10 = 6.$	$66 \div 11 = 6.$	$72 \div 12 = 6.$
$63 \div 9 = 7.$	$70 \div 10 = 7.$	$77 \div 11 = 7.$	$84 \div 12 = 7.$
$72 \div 9 = 8.$	$80 \div 10 = 8.$	$88 \div 11 = 8.$	$96 \div 12 = 8.$
$81 \div 9 = 9.$	$90 \div 10 = 9.$	$99 \div 11 = 9.$	$108 \div 12 = 9.$

ORAL EXERCISES.

I.

$6 \div 2 = ?$	$14 \div 2 = ?$	$24 \div 8 = ?$	$48 \div 6 = ?$
$8 \div 1 = ?$	$18 \div 3 = ?$	$28 \div 4 = ?$	$45 \div 5 = ?$
$9 \div 9 = ?$	$16 \div 4 = ?$	$20 \div 5 = ?$	$48 \div 12 = ?$
$4 \div 2 = ?$	$15 \div 3 = ?$	$32 \div 4 = ?$	$44 \div 11 = ?$
$6 \div 3 = ?$	$12 \div 2 = ?$	$30 \div 6 = ?$	$49 \div 7 = ?$
$8 \div 4 = ?$	$12 \div 3 = ?$	$35 \div 7 = ?$	$56 \div 8 = ?$
$9 \div 3 = ?$	$18 \div 2 = ?$	$36 \div 9 = ?$	$50 \div 10 = ?$
$8 \div 2 = ?$	$25 \div 5 = ?$	$32 \div 8 = ?$	$54 \div 9 = ?$
$7 \div 1 = ?$	$24 \div 4 = ?$	$36 \div 6 = ?$	$64 \div 8 = ?$
$6 \div 6 = ?$	$27 \div 3 = ?$	$40 \div 5 = ?$	$63 \div 7 = ?$

II.

$\frac{16}{2} = ?$	$\frac{27}{9} = ?$	$\frac{72}{8} = ?$	$\frac{10}{2} = ?$
$\frac{4}{1} = ?$	$\frac{28}{8} = ?$	$\frac{81}{9} = ?$	$\frac{54}{6} = ?$
$\frac{8}{8} = ?$	$\frac{30}{5} = ?$	$\frac{44}{12} = ?$	$\frac{48}{8} = ?$
$\frac{24}{6} = ?$	$\frac{33}{11} = ?$	$\frac{36}{12} = ?$	$\frac{72}{8} = ?$
$\frac{36}{4} = ?$	$\frac{36}{6} = ?$	$\frac{48}{8} = ?$	$\frac{40}{5} = ?$
$\frac{24}{6} = ?$	$\frac{42}{7} = ?$	$\frac{30}{10} = ?$	$\frac{60}{10} = ?$
$\frac{20}{4} = ?$	$\frac{46}{9} = ?$	$\frac{10}{5} = ?$	$\frac{42}{7} = ?$
$\frac{18}{6} = ?$	$\frac{54}{7} = ?$	$\frac{44}{11} = ?$	$\frac{77}{7} = ?$
$\frac{14}{7} = ?$	$\frac{48}{12} = ?$	$\frac{60}{10} = ?$	$\frac{18}{9} = ?$

III.

15÷5= ?	23÷3= ?	57÷10= ?	82÷10= ?
16÷5= ?	10÷4= ?	73÷ 8= ?	74÷11= ?
12÷6= ?	42÷8= ?	66÷ 7= ?	35÷ 4= ?
14÷6= ?	17÷6= ?	69÷ 8= ?	27÷ 4= ?
21÷7= ?	12÷7= ?	95÷11= ?	99÷12= ?
24÷7= ?	19÷3= ?	87÷12= ?	55÷ 7= ?
40÷8= ?	25÷6= ?	65÷ 9= ?	81÷12= ?
46÷8= ?	34÷5= ?	18÷11= ?	75÷ 9= ?
18÷9= ?	43÷5= ?	44÷ 7= ?	63÷10= ?
26÷9= ?	53÷9= ?	58÷ 9= ?	51÷ 6= ?

IV.

22÷2= ?	93÷3= ?	48÷3= ?	78÷7= ?
36÷3= ?	68÷2= ?	75÷5= ?	43÷3= ?
48÷4= ?	50÷5= ?	60÷5= ?	61÷4= ?
55÷5= ?	66÷6= ?	96÷8= ?	79÷5= ?
88÷4= ?	86÷2= ?	84÷7= ?	75÷4= ?
28÷2= ?	84÷4= ?	91÷7= ?	94÷6= ?
46÷2= ?	63÷3= ?	78÷6= ?	82÷7= ?
69÷3= ?	96÷8= ?	85÷5= ?	33÷2= ?
77÷7= ?	44÷2= ?	42÷4= ?	47÷3= ?
64÷2= ?	99÷9= ?	51÷3= ?	58÷4= ?

V.

Give quotients and remainders at sight :

A. 8)13 8)26 8)95 8)71 8)83 8)66 8)51

B. 8)39 8)47 8)12 8)35 8)77 8)56 8)27

C. 8)11 8)30 8)89 8)90 8)41 8)62 8)19

D. 8)86 8)52 8)39 8)43 8)65 8)41 8)44

NOTE.—The last exercises are extended as follows : All the numbers from 11 to 99 are arranged without order, and in columns and
lines, and each of the nine digits is taken successively as a divisor.

VI.

$(12+ 6)\div 3= ?$	$(37+16)\div 9= ?$	$(6\times9)\div7= ?$
$(20+ 4)\div12= ?$	$(29-13)\div 6= ?$	$48\div(2\times6)= ?$
$(17+11)\div 2= ?$	$(48- 7)\div11= ?$	$36\div(3\times4)= ?$
$(26- 6)\div 4= ?$	$(7\times 6)\div 3= ?$	$72\div(4\times2)= ?$
$(18- 8)\div 2= ?$	$(8\times 9)\div 6= ?$	$64\div(3\times2)= ?$
$(47- 5)\div 6= ?$	$(6\times 4)\div 2= ?$	$96\div(8\times3)= ?$
$(19+17)\div 5= ?$	$(5\times 8)\div 4= ?$	$84\div(3\times4)= ?$

$(18- 6)\div(4+2)= ?$	$(47- 7)\div(3\times1)= ?$
$(36- 9)\div(1+4)= ?$	$(93- 8)\div(6\times2)= ?$
$(84- 4)\div(3+7)= ?$	$(43+ 7)\div(3\times5)= ?$
$(63- 8)\div(11-6)= ?$	$(48+12)\div(6\times4)= ?$
$(76+12)\div(14-3)= ?$	$(8\times 9)\div(4\times3)= ?$
$(36+ 7)\div(8-1)= ?$	$(72\div 6)\div(9+1)= ?$
$(42+23)\div(3+2)= ?$	$(8\times11)\div(3+6)= ?$
$(86+ 4)\div(6+3)= ?$	$(7\times 9)\div(17-3)= ?$
$(7\times 8)\div(4\times2)= ?$	$(78\div 6)\div(3\times4)= ?$
$(8\times 9)\div(4\times3)= ?$	$(93\div 3)\div(72\div9)= ?$

VII.

1. At 4 cents apiece, how many oranges can be bought
for 16 cents ? 28 cents ? 32 cents ? 20 cents ? 8 cents?

2. A man earns $2 a day. How long will it take him
to earn $18 ? $4 ? $6 ? $12 ? $2 ?

3. How many yards of muslin can be bought for 72
cents, at 6 cents a yard ? 8 cents? 12 cents ? 9 cents ?

4. How many times can 5 yards of cloth be taken from
a piece containing 25 yards ? 45 yards ? 60 yards ? 30
yards ?

5. By writing 8 lines a day, how many days will it take John to write 56 lines? 16 lines? 64 lines? 88 lines? 40 lines?

6. At 11 cents a pound, how many pounds of sugar can be bought for 88 cents? 55 cents? 99 cents? 22 cents? 66 cents? 44 cents?

7. If one man can do a piece of work in 36 days, how long will it take 9 men to do it? 4 men? 6 men? 3 men'? 8 men?

8. Divide 24 into 3 equal parts. Into 6 equal parts.

9. How many dozen of eggs, at 9 cents a dozen, can be bought for $1.08? 81 cents? 63 cents? 99 cents?

10. There are 4 quarts in a gallon; how many gallons in 36 quarts? 48 quarts? 12 quarts? 44 quarts?

11. From a farm containing 110 acres, how many lots of 10 acres each can be sold?

12. How many sheep, at $7 a head, can be bought for $49? $21? $14? $35? $63?

13. There are 12 months in a year; how many years in 84 months? 60 months? 120 months?

14. In what number of days will a man travel 30 miles, at the rate of 5 miles a day?

15. How many times 9 are 6 times 12?

16. At $2 apiece, how many hats can be purchased for $32? $48? $72? $86?

17. Mr. Johnson travelled 140 miles in 7 days. How many miles did he travel each day?

18. How many barrels of apples, at $3 a barrel, can be purchased for $72? . $65? $39?

19. A farmer bought sheep for $60, at the rate of $4 a head. How many did he buy?

20. How many barrels of flour can be sold for $120, at $8 per barrel?

21. How often is 5 contained in 75 ?   95 ?   60 ?

22. If 9 barrels of flour cost $63, what will 7 barrels cost ?   6 barrels ?   4 barrels ?

23. If a man earn $55 in 5 weeks, how much will he earn in 11 weeks ?

24. If 8 yards of cloth cost $48, what will 12 yards cost ?   16 yards ?   9 yards ?   14 yards ?

25. What will 5 tons of hay cost, if 2 tons cost $26 ? $18 ? $30 ? $36 ?

26. How many bottles of mucilage, at 10 cents a bottle, will pay for 40 copies at 4 cents each ?

27. At the rate of 28 miles in 7 hours, how far would a man travel in 20 hours?   11 hours ?   14 hours ?

28. How many bedsteads, at $6 each, can be bought for 11 boxes of oranges at $6 each, and $18 worth of lemons ?

29. How many fancy lead-pencils, at 9 cents each, will pay for 5 tops at 6 cents each, and 11 three-cent stamps ?

30. How many times can a father divide $90 among his three sons, giving each $5 every time ?

VIII.

1. $5 \times 4, \div 2, + 7, - 3, \times 6, - 24, + 6, \div 11, + 4 = ?$

2. $3 + 13, \times 5, - 60, - 5, \times 3, + 4, \div 7, - 2, + 8, \times 3 = ?$

3. $27 - 3, \div 8, + 9, \times 6, - 50, \times 3, - 16, + 25, \div 3 = ?$

4. $48 \div 6, + 3, \times 9, + 1, \div 10, - 4, \times 13, - 8, \div 7 = ?$

5. $144 \div 12, - 1, \times 11, - 13, \div 9, - 5, \times 6, \div 3 = ?$

6. $7 \times 9, - 3, \div 4, + 3, \times 3, - 4, \times 2, - 19, \div 9 = ?$

7. $36 + 9, \div 5, \times 2, \div 3, + 4, \times 5, - 25, \div 5, + 6 = ?$

8. $21 + 9, \times 4, - 10, \div 11, + 16, \div 2, - 3, - 1, \times 9 = ?$

9. $108 \div 12, + 11, + 4, \div 4, + 1, \times 7, - 4, \div 3, \times 7 = ?$

10. $86 - 31, \div 11, + 17, - 4, \div 9, + 7, \times 4, + 11, - 2 = ?$

SHORT DIVISION.

1. Divide 9767 by 9.

OPERATION.

$$9\,\underline{)\,9767}$$
$$1085\tfrac{2}{9}$$

SOLUTION.—9 is contained in 9 thousands 1 thousand times, with no remainder.

9 into 7 hundreds is contained 0 hundred times. Annexing the 7 hundreds to the 6 tens, we have 76 tens, which, divided by 9, gives 8 tens for quotient, and a remainder of 4 tens.

The 4 tens annexed to the 7 units make 47 units. 9 into 47 units is contained 5 units times, with a remainder of 2 units. Hence, the quotient of 9767 divided by 9 is $1085\frac{2}{9}$.

PROOF.—Multiply the quotient by the divisor, and to the product add the remainder; the result should be equal to the dividend.

ILLUSTRATIONS.

	2.	*3.*	*4.*	*5.*
	4) 672	6) 287	7) 903	8) 8145
Ans.	168	$47\frac{5}{6}$	129	$1018\frac{1}{8}$
	168	47	129	1018
	4	6	7	8
Proof,	672	282	903	8144
		+ 5		+ 1
		287		8145

WRITTEN EXERCISES.

6. 840÷4.	*12.* 616÷7.	*18.* 472÷4.	*24.* 718÷7.
7. 950÷5.	*13.* 555÷3.	*19.* 938÷3.	*25.* 396÷9.
8. 834÷6.	*14.* 711÷9.	*20.* 477÷2.	*26.* 482÷6.
9. 399÷7.	*15.* 736÷8.	*21.* 631÷3.	*27.* 307÷4.
10. 441÷9.	*16.* 879÷5.	*22.* 976÷8.	*28.* 603÷9.
11. 392÷8.	*17.* 384÷6.	*23.* 504÷4.	*29.* 500÷8.

30. 2735÷7.	*38.* 5837÷4.	*46.* 2782÷7.
31. 8945÷6.	*39.* 4002÷3.	*47.* 4906÷2.
32. 2147÷8.	*40.* 7000÷5.	*48.* 7580÷8.
33. 6092÷9.	*41.* 9000÷7.	*49.* 3355÷6.
34. 8070÷8.	*42.* 4500÷6.	*50.* 7415÷9.
35. 6439÷6.	*43.* 1801÷9.	*51.* 8000÷6.
36. 8296÷7.	*44.* 3400÷8.	*52.* 4010÷3.
37. 7350÷5.	*45.* 7030÷4.	*53.* 2030÷7.

54. 73504÷8.	*59.* 93007÷3.	*64.* 8291÷6.
55. 24319÷9.	*60.* 86214÷5.	*65.* 4918÷7.
56. 36848÷6.	*61.* 53720÷9.	*66.* 5762÷8.
57. 20895÷5.	*62.* 38808÷3.	*67.* 3015÷9.
58. 49763÷7.	*63.* 10738÷4.	*68.* 8223÷5.

69. 34760511÷8.	*73.* 47642001÷4.	*77.* 60000023÷7.
70. 47984111÷9.	*74.* 37400010÷6.	*78.* 95121351÷5.
71. 74653485÷2.	*75.* 90437281÷9.	*79.* 66600177÷4.
72. 60700840÷5.	*76.* 27834422÷8.	*80.* 38842239÷8.

81. 10945718809411÷7.	*91.* 39988866044031÷3.
82. 25814100635618÷3.	*92.* 73564125659750÷9.
83. 78754532124415÷6.	*93.* 81213098642533÷5.
84. 23500077131417÷8.	*94.* 66100034587778÷6.
85. 35611267329688÷9.	*95.* 49223432567892÷7.
86. 43121952146324÷7.	*96.* 12000000115050÷2.
87. 56131789425811÷5.	*97.* 48009133300161÷8.
88. 24581900456388÷8.	*98.* 23250490110111÷9.
89. 79625553172410÷6.	*99.* 78356797443119÷6.
90. 80170940260067÷4.	*100.* 57005700067800÷5.

101. 12740807196041÷9.	*103.* 11100022244455÷8.
102. 60094315817935÷7.	*104.* 90980860650039÷5.

LONG DIVISION.

1. Divide 231435 by 38.

OPERATION.

38) 231435 (6090
228
———
    343
    342
    ———
     15

SOLUTION.—38 into 231 thousands are contained 6 thousands times. 6 thousands times 38 are 228 thousands, which, subtracted from 231 thousands, leave 3 thousands.

Annexing the 4 hundreds to the 3 thousands, we get 34 hundreds. 38 are not contained in 34 hundreds any hundreds times. A cipher is therefore written in hundreds' place in the quotient, and the 3 tens annexed to the remainder.

38 into 343 tens are contained 9 tens times, with a remainder of 1 ten, which, with the 5 units annexed, make 15 units.

38 into 15 units are not contained any units times. Hence, 38 into 231435 are contained 6090 times, with a remainder of 15.

NOTE.—When there are ciphers at the right of the divisor, omit them, and cut off an equal number of figures from the right of the dividend. Then divide the remainder of the dividend by the remaining figures of the divisor. For the final remainder, annex to the particular remainder the figures cut off from the dividend.

ILLUSTRATIONS.

2. Divide 1062934 by 306, and prove it.

OPERATION.

Divisor. Dividend. Quotient.

306) 1062934 (3473
918
————
1449
1224
————
2253
2142
————
1114
 918
————
Remainder, 196

PROOF.

   3473 Quotient.
    306 Divisor.
————
  20838
10419
————
1062738
    196 Remainder.
————
1062934 Dividend.

WRITTEN EXERCISES.

3. 888÷37.	*11.* 608÷38.	*19.* 364÷29.
4. 936÷52.	*12.* 894÷76.	*20.* 604÷54.
5. 975÷25.	*13.* 247÷19.	*21.* 477÷53.
6. 456÷24.	*14.* 493÷27.	*22.* 836÷44.
7. 924÷33.	*15.* 816÷81.	*23.* 520÷36.
8. 546÷13.	*16.* 306÷18.	*24.* 700÷68.
9. 804÷67.	*17.* 537÷46.	*25.* 930÷85.
10. 946÷43.	*18.* 732÷61.	*26.* 800÷57.

27. 4219÷49.	*33.* 7581÷47.	*39.* 2191÷67.
28. 1335÷15.	*34.* 3544÷93.	*40.* 7932÷48.
29. 1617÷21.	*35.* 6450÷25.	*41.* 2379÷62.
30. 1081÷23.	*36.* 8643÷34.	*42.* 3116÷37.
31. 6184÷58.	*37.* 8864÷92.	*43.* 1205÷31.
32. 8476÷83.	*38.* 5621÷77.	*44.* 8329÷64.

45. 5000÷49.	*51.* 3000÷44.	*57.* 9070÷29.
46. 8000÷22.	*52.* 8000÷71.	*58.* 3040÷34.
47. 7000÷38.	*53.* 1000÷88.	*59.* 8090÷41.
48. 9000÷76.	*54.* 4000÷68.	*60.* 5100÷65.
49. 6000÷54.	*55.* 9000÷33.	*61.* 8210÷93.
50. 4000÷97.	*56.* 7000÷77.	*62.* 6380÷79.

63. 38584÷53.	*68.* 36501÷95.	*73.* 83915÷27.
64. 70308÷37.	*69.* 85222÷24.	*74.* 99098÷43.
65. 10166÷26.	*70.* 93128÷37.	*75.* 20919÷82.
66. 13314÷42.	*71.* 54236÷71.	*76.* 53714÷68.
67. 74099÷83.	*72.* 60119÷86.	*77.* 68328÷74.

78. 638922127251÷34.	*80.* 992873419201÷92.
79. 577375898704÷15.	*81.* 712749921494÷73.

82. 105197150448÷46.
83. 125543744550÷17.
84. 132928677666÷68.
85. 157581180652÷19.
86. 107561287080÷33.
87. 139174863803÷94.

88. 231603688965÷23.
89. 796491867798÷29.
90. 524870227218÷96.
91. 508906968145÷68.
92. 533913126274÷79.
93. 807414826243÷84.

94. 73898÷126.
95. 60584÷243.
96. 51084÷396.
97. 46219÷627.
98. 74670÷108.
99. 88561÷913.

100. 69723÷420.
101. 80080÷572.
102. 14513÷307.
103. 50480÷208.
104. 35047÷320.
105. 14368÷462.

106. 736219÷981.
107. 692534÷645.
108. 830654÷472.
109. 755391÷828.
110. 363007÷483.
111. 908405÷674.

112. 574654876÷610.
113. 376457087÷450.
114. 160075840÷200.
115. 757807059÷190.
116. 900003940÷300.
117. 781900630÷400.
118. 847008395÷530.
119. 941837062÷710.

120. 600901870÷500.
121. 750806037÷700.
122. 112007914÷800.
123. 502904300÷900.
124. 894013000÷390.
125. 340215680÷400.
126. 612107998÷600.
127. 900003400÷370.

128. 807436587÷659.
129. 706594876÷337.
130. 801970007÷971.
131. 954761827÷684.
132. 162457830÷294.
133. 679596891÷876.
134. 434079081÷576.
135. 847695876÷341.
136. 946807075÷279.
137. 757806920÷196.

138. 307444005÷835.
139. 188088128÷397.
140. 300451692÷284.
141. 724309515÷172.
142. 936245261÷293.
143. 710321293÷408.
144. 900886241÷528.
145. 162730041÷601.
146. 890730566÷792.
147. 209804367÷271.

148. 8271607810125÷115.

149. 2105079103532÷127.

150. 1116982596600÷135.

151. 5526095892204÷142.

152. 9762094146828÷139.

153. 1161728053825÷195.

154. 1351441556271÷183.

155. 6127759222395÷173.

156. 101097166410÷264.

157. 145137140415÷379.

158. 409144746134÷874.

159. 293059314196÷786.

160. 348541256471÷485.

161. 763149152094÷350.

162. 810920730251÷694.

163. 683271418314÷852.

164. 4361720÷5060.

165. 2406000÷6000.

166. 9120900÷7100.

167. 8974300÷8070.

168. 1784010÷2050.

169. 5831507÷4000.

170. 3711420÷6873.

171. 1220313÷4503.

172. 1395940÷3068.

173. 2462776÷3709.

174. 2985920÷6020.

175. 4597800÷7663.

176. 8292779÷9083.

177. 7479680÷7540.

178. 6301372÷6314.

179. 9163128÷4718.

180. 4272093÷5719.

181. 5612143÷3716.

182. 533248560612÷4321.

183. 525807970480÷8762.

184. 172359899942÷4208.

185. 673950034116÷6319.

186. 103216784879÷2647.

187. 796835432738÷3385.

188. 493200704008÷8296.

189. 506700418006÷7309.

190. 961417517759÷4513.

191. 724009316738÷6519.

192. 836127200591÷7315.

193. 102769671303÷3879.

194. 6892003599351479÷307534.

195. 1121139009326201÷635471.

196. 3689789656280676÷569946.

197. 1107869602259673÷279873.

198. 2688395691108992÷386972.

199. 1159952417443311÷198647.

200. 2176066225367412÷498764.

201. 4008170747932649÷698471.

UNITED STATES CURRENCY.

26. Reduce the dividend to cents, if necessary, and divide as in simple numbers. The quotient will be the answer in cents ; which may be reduced to dollars and cents by placing the separating point two places from the right.

27. When both dividend and divisor are in currency, reduce each to cents if necessary, and divide as in simple numbers. The quotient will be the required number.

ILLUSTRATIONS.

1. Divide $187 equally among 13 men.

2. For $600 how many barrels of flour can be bought at $7.50 per barrel?

```
         1.                        2.
   Cents.    Cents.      $7.50 ) $600.00 ( 80 barrels.
13 ) $187.00 ( 1438             6000
      13         or             ----
      --                           0
      57       $14.38
      52
      --
      50
      39
      --
      110
      104
      ---
       6
```

WRITTEN EXERCISES.

3. Divide $396.76 by 28. *Ans.* $14.17.
4. Divide $1308.24 by 79. *Ans.* $16.56.
5. Divide $6048 by 108. *Ans.* $56.

6. Divide $37806.29 by 392. *Ans.* $96.44.

7. Divide $99.88 by 11 cents. *Ans.* 908.

8. Divide $137.97 by 63 cents. *Ans.* 219.

9. Divide $15275 by $325. *Ans.* 47.

10. Divide $9672 by $806. *Ans.* 12.

11. Divide $9003.75 by $3.75. *Ans.* 2401.

.12. Divide $276.00 by $9.20. *Ans.* 30.

13. If 63 acres of land cost $7938, what will 1 acre cost ? *Ans.* $126.

14. If 516 chairs cost $2012.40, what will 1 chair cost ? *Ans.* $3.90.

15. How much a head will I pay for sheep, if 280 cost $840.00 ? *Ans.* $3.00.

16. What is the price of butter per pound, when 300 pounds cost $105? *Ans.* 35¢.

17. At $9.25 a ton, how many tons of coal can be purchased for $120.25 ? *Ans.* 13 tons.

18. How many baskets of peaches can be bought for $6, at 25 cents per basket ? *Ans.* 24 baskets.

19. Bought a barrel of vinegar for $13.23, at the rate of 21 cents a gallon. How many gallons in the barrel ?

Ans. 63 gallons.

20. How much does a laborer receive per day, if for 42 days he earn $56.70 ? *Ans.* $1.35.

21. At $7 a barrel, how many barrels of flour can be bought for $273 ? *Ans.* 39 barrels.

22. How many yards of cloth can be purchased for $633.50, at $3.62 per yard ? *Ans.* 175 yards.

23. During a voyage of 45 days a vessel burns 1620 tons of coal. How many tons does she burn per day ?

Ans. 36 tons.

24. What is the price per acre of a farm of 2114 acres, that costs $126840 ? *Ans.* $60.

WRITTEN REVIEW.

1. A farmer bought a horse for $225, and a carriage for $140. He sold both for $450. How much did he gain? *Ans.* $85.

2. There are 23680 yards of cloth in 320 pieces. How many yards in each piece? *Ans.* 74 yards.

3. If a tailor requires 3 days to make a suit of clothes, how long will it take him to make 426 suits?

4. There are 5280 feet in a mile. How many steps of 2 feet each will a boy take in travelling 8 miles?

5. A father gave each of his 3 sons $12500, and each of his 2 daughters $13000. How much more did the sons receive than the daughters? *Ans.* $11500.

6. If 1870 suits of clothes cost $48620, what will one suit cost? *Ans.* $26.

7. If 3 horses cost $540, what will 9 horses cost at the same rate? *Ans.* $1620.

8. I have 9630 pounds of tea which I wish to pack in 30 chests. How many pounds must be put in each chest? *Ans.* 321 pounds.

9. Find the cost of 140 barrels of potatoes, at $2.75 a barrel. *Ans.* $315.

10. How many pounds of sugar, at 10 cents a pound, will pay for 15 dozen of eggs at 20 cents a dozen?

11. At $58 an acre, how many acres of land can be bought for $1226555? How much money will be left?

12. By selling a farm of 175 acres for $12270, I gained $1422. How much did it cost me per acre?
Ans. $62.

13. Bought a farm for $3792, which was 3 times as much as a house cost me. How much did the house cost? *Ans.* $1264.

14. Find the cost of 60 pounds of butter, at 32 cents a pound, and 45 pounds of tea at 50 cents a pound.
Ans. $41.70.

15. I bought 16 cows at $39 each, and 34 oxen at $53 each. How much did I pay for all? *Ans.* $2426.

16. A farmer sold 184 bushels of wheat at $1.25 a bushel, and expended the amount received in buying sheep at $5 a head. How many sheep did he buy?
Ans. 46 sheep.

17. Bought 54 barrels of flour for $324. For what must it be sold a barrel to gain $162? *Ans.* $9.

18. What number multiplied by 83209 will produce 10983588? *Ans.* 132.

19. A merchant expended $564 in purchasing boots at $6 a pair, which he afterwards sold at $8 a pair. How much did he gain? *Ans.* $188.

20. Bought 18 hogsheads of sugar at $34 a hogshead, and sold it for $42 a hogshead. What was gained?
Ans. $144.

21. If 8 men can build a house in 124 days, how long would it take one man to build it? *Ans.* 992 days. .

22. A coal merchant bought some coal for $180 and sold it for $210, gaining $1.50 on each ton. How many tons did he buy? *Ans.* 20 tons.

23. A grocer buys some potatoes, for which he pays $1023.70. He sells them at $1.37 per bushel, and gains $17.50. How many bushels are there?
Ans. 760 bushels.

24. Multiply 864723 by 327, and divide the product by 109. *Ans.* 2594169.

25. Sold 6 oxen at $75 each, 4 horses at $265 each, a carriage for $325, and a plow for $25. How much did I receive for the whole? *Ans.* $1860.

ANSWERS.

Page 9.

I.

1. 1882.
2. 3904.
3. 2009.
   6008.
4. 1863.
5. 7541.
6. 9047.
   505.
7. 6384.
8. 9127.
9. 6589.
10. 3105.
11. 1122.
12. 1355.
13. 8897.
14. 6340.
15. 8896.
16. 4871.
17. 5006.
    9050.
18. 3945.
19. 8030.
    4004.
20. 2987.

II.

21. 31200.
22. 70084.
23. 87006.
24. 10001.
    7002.
25. 20202.
26. 15840.
27. 12317.
28. 25809.
29. 63701.
30. 44963.
31. 76810.

32. 99425.
33. 86999.
34. 61002.
    60000.
35. 10010.
    15000.

Page 10.

III.

36. 806907.
37. 527802.
    912000.
38. 625900.
39. 612136.
    100026.
40. 900006.
41. 121319.
    510000.
42. 800000.
43. 825008.
44. 611094.
45. 940030.
46. 809000.
47. 161784.
    320000.
48. 391211.
    982000.
49. 199999.
    206000.
50. 644900.

Page 15.

II.

26. 8658.
27. 2187.
28. 9375.
29. 1719.
30. 6439.
31. 4998.
32. 3542.
33. 7400.

34. 5802.
35. 6209.
36. 8300.
37. 9018.
38. 7203.
39. 4002.
    1005.
40. 9012.
    2008.
41. 6040.
    9031.
42. 1474.
43. 5113.
44. 2014.
    9003.
45. 4002.
    6050.

Page 16.

III.

46. 15131.
47. 16245.
48. 11333.
49. 19406.
50. 12602.
51. 10010.
    7003.
52. 13000.
    8013.
53. 17000.
    3006.
54. 20020.
    6002.
55. 41234.
56. 20409.
57. 41560.
58. 39702.
59. 84208.
60. 71030.
    1001.

IV.

61. 100300.
62. 200506.
63. 600910.
64. 912206.
65. 304102.
66. 861014.
67. 153975.
    230000.
68. 212869.
    506000.
69. 722096.
70. 401025.
71. 900000.
    402000.
    903000.
72. 300100.
73. 703509.
74. 400004.
    500000.
    900006.
75. 116412.

Page 17.

V.

76. 4610499.
77. 9822704.
78. 6900175.
    5700000.
79. 8012060.
80. 7016040.
81. 10003071.
82. 15203600.
    8604000.
83. 17800506.
    9309000.
84. 24012090.
85. 41007030.
86. 86300100.
    76200000.

87. 54000000.
68000020.
46000020.
88. 65032021.
57044000.
89. 29170462.
90. 218946394.
91. 720912235.
92. 607042050.
300010000.

93. 100200300.
300006000.
94. 960004040.
95. 410600200.
205001000.
96. 13001020.
97. 60000007.
5000003.
98. 18000009.
300000030.
6000933.

99. 3011010080.
100. 120014010071.
101. 257009064042.
102. 432090003025.
103. 676256074067.
104. 6009002046.
105. 94179065483.
106. 79097344028.
107. 656842799.
108. 896045009841.

Page 32.
I.

1. 679.
2. 999.
3. 401.
4. 883.
5. 694.
6. 887.
7. 784.
8. 690.
9. 690.
10. 998.
11. 772.
12. 890.
13. 880.
14. 980.
15. 991.
16. 875.
17. 974.
18. 590.
19. 693.
20. 895.
21. 666.
22. 793.
23. 636.
24. 453.
25. 864.
26. 783.
27. 875.
28. 437.
29. 464.
30. 758.
31. 754.
32. 821.
33. 471.
34. 461.

35. 525.
36. 746.
37. 771.
38. 801.
39. 721.
40. 1033.
41. 857.
42. 853.
43. 1211.
44. 1509.
45. 534.
46. 1290.
47. 1840.
48. 1223.
49. 1306.
50. 1000.
51. 851.
52. 1300.
53. 727.
54. 1378.
55. 1288.
56. 1008.
57. 1345.
58. 1504.
59. 821.
60. 939.
61. 1110.
62. 1555.
63. 1269.

Page 33.
II.

1. 1101.
2. 1165.
3. 1580.
4. 1207.

5. 1209.
6. 1604.
7. 968.
8. 1438.
9. 2192.
10. 1465.
11. 1348.
12. 1243.
13. 1187.
14. 1992.
15. 1339.
16. 1673.
17. 2230.
18. 2401.
19. 1875.
20. 1185.
21. 1122.
22. 1943.
23. 2140.
24. 2048.

Page 34.
III.

1. 14814.
2. 25926.
3. 18073.
4. 15731.
5. 16346.
6. 13672.
7. 6993.
8. 15082.
9. 15184.
10. 9015.
11. 32690.
12. 39163.
13. 25406.

14. 52563.
15. 35671.

Page 35.
IV.

1. 435.
2. 1538.
3. 828.
4. 1196.
5. 1480.
6. 925.
7. 2087.
8. 1016.
9. 1569.
10. 1677.
11. 1042.
12. 1052.
13. 2035.
14. 399.
15. 1305.
16. 445.
17. 1291.
18. 314.
19. 767.
20. 532.
21. 899.
22. 780.
23. 2219.
24. 2018.

Page 36.
V.

9. 8272.
10. 2155.
11. 1640.
12. 1421.

13. 1690.
14. 1072.
15. 14395.
16. 23566.
17. 17972.
18. 19196.
19. 26018.

Page 37.
VI.

1. 71424.
2. 175971.
3. 86428.
4. 161150.
5. 200243.
6. 153148.
7. 185971.
8. 224152.
9. 134696.
10. 260045.
11. 252241.
12. 232726.
13. 109322.
14. 222109.
15. 194962.
16. 1644718.
17. 1463290.
18. 1466661.
19. 889649.
20. 233251.

Page 38.
VII.

4. 806256.
5. 255956.
7. 109444.
8. 301899.
9. 1297688.
10. 1014475.
11. 2199316.
12. 2190531.
13. 426716.

Page 40.
VIII.

1. 1605.
2. 4240.
3. 3463.

4. 3172.
5. 3261.
6. 34922.
7. 37529.
8. 51104.
9. 37049.
10. 42476.
11. 58991.
12. 41452.
13. 53574.
14. 40402.
15. 48152.

Page 41.
IX.

1. 5029.
2. 5239.
3. 5584.
4. 5997.
5. 5949.
6. 6042.
7. 3302.
8. 4481.
9. 33796.
10. 37280.
11. 19412.
12. 116575.
13. 164936.
14. 157651.
15. 213866.
16. 75552.
17. 546119.
18. 710663.
19. 514569.
20. 629286.
21. 184294.

Page 42.
X.

1. 8613.
2. 17386.
3. 662993.
4. 10704.
5. 101790.
6. 257940.
7. 769115602.
8. 333603732.
9. 24054.

10. 2314113.
11. 23421.
12. 259335.
13. 245024.
14. 118546.
15. 1476987.
16. 2613496.
17. 1722626.
18. 955987.
19. 605096.
20. 4300906.
21. 568401.
22. 23690659.
23. 70834948.
24. 687497442.

Page 43.

1. $4.39.
2. $12.22.
3. $64.75.
4. $81.10.
5. $0.15.
   $0.37.
   $0.11.
6. $0.50.
   $0.45.
   $0.16.
7. $0.28.
   $0.43.
8. $13.16.
9. $36.56.
10. $84.92.
11. $68.11.
12. $23.48.
13. $93.62.
14. $41.28.
15. $84.29.
16. $51.19.
17. $0.03.
   $0.09.
   $25.00.
18. $0.34.
   $0.79.
19. $0.28.
   $0.14.
20. $0.38.
   $0.70.

Page 44.

2. $20.53.
3. $30.90.
4. $18.27.
5. $26.72.
6. $949.87.
7. $1382.48.
8. $545.36.
9. $1766.07.
10. $83309.57.
11. $409501.11.
12. $1098302.44.
13. $16045.33.
14. $15131.05.
15. $14286.51.
16. $21454.65.
17. $1125.81.
18. $6503.52.
19. $203.35.
20. $2807.79.
21. $71.98.
22. $1895.50.
23. $51.50.
24. $4768.00.
25. $4605.75.
26. $1147.38

Page 46.

1. Mon. 1858.
   Tues. 2932.
   Wed. 3307.
   Thurs. 2521.
   Fri. 4458.
   Sat. 3828.
   Papers, 8819.
   Magazines, 4874.
   Fiction, 2053.
   Science, 1428.
   Poetry, 1039.
   Religion, 1690.
   Total, 19904.
2. Mon. 27310.
   Tues. 12988.
   Wed. 13543.
   Thurs. 13214.
   Fri. 15000.
   Sat. 29383.

Ordinary Letters, 49227.
Registered Letters, 2846.
Postals, 15369.
Books, 4523.
Packages, 1450.
Papers, 38023.
Total, 111438.
3. Mon. $620.12.
Tues. $1740.00.
Wed. $2401.41.
Thurs. $2454.03.
Fri. $792.15.
Sat. $1609.88.
1st Wk, $864.05.
2d " $622.18.
3d " $1602.66.
4th " $1438.10.
5th " $913.06.
6th " $1006.28.
7th " $1085.57.
8th " $744.77.
9th " $1340.92.
Total, $9617.59.
4. Tea, 7745.
Coffee, 11076.
Sugar, 25146.
Flour, 42904.
Butter, 16588.
Cheese, 11468.
Jan. 7830.
Feb. 4036.
Mar. 6167.
April, 7281.
May, 10817.
June, 10370.
July, 9925.
Aug. 10318.
Sept. 10915.
Oct. 17093.
Nov. 9585.
Dec. 10590.
Total, 114927.
5. Jan. $4739.99.
Feb. $4209.41.
Mar. $4421.54.
April, $4579.07.

May, $4766.63.
June, $5317.87.
1st Sec. $7556.50.
2d " $5576.98.
3d " $4613.79.
4th " $3832.60.
5th " $2391.50.
6th " $800.02.
7th " $798.36.
8th " $2434.76.
Total, $38034.51.

Page 48.
6. $3.87.
7. 15584.
8. $1485.
9. $4776.
10. 383.
12. 960 trees.
14. $16.52.
15. $4492.25.
16. 21973 bushels.
17. 35564 feet.
18. 3441 bushels.
19. $2275.15.
20. 338 marbles.

Page 60.
6. 524.
7. 25.
8. 235.
9. 84.
10. 123.
11. 118.
12. 519.
13. 158.
14. 284.
15. 54.
16. 379.
17. 188.
18. 187.
19. 196.
20. 179.
21. 223.
22. 755.
23. 391.
24. 88.
25. 155.

26. 3505.
27. 2151.
28. 2080.
29. 6469.
30. 5542.
31. 6251.
32. 114.
33. 4123.
34. 4617.
35. 7189.
36. 2225.
37. 2994.
38. 106.
39. 3772.
40. 508.
41. 119.
42. 3075.
43. 812.
44. 2037.
45. 212.
46. 149.
47. 86.
48. 45.
49. 467.
50. 55.
51. 511.
52. 311.
53. 75.
54. 397.
55. 188.
56. 293.
57. 717.
58. 486.
59. 48928.
60. 1298. ·
61. 307.
62. 1855.
63. 103.
64. 204.
65. 55.
66. 66103.
67. 526.
68. 66.
69. 1356.
70. 5259.
71. 4424.
72. 1928.
73. 34813.

74. 59792.
75. 11995.
76. 29011.
77. 21965.
78. 1.
79. 57992.
80. 82203.
81. 2884.
82. 35147.
83. 23916.
84. 77232.
85. 15479.
86. 12596.
87. 344208.
88. 380332.
89. 449647.
90. 401338.
91. 544287.
92. 638092.
93. 134596.
94. 41340.
95. 172638.
96. 190794.
97. 91799.
98. 111110.
99. 455486.
100. 377964.
101. 181129.
102. 425915.
103. 762889.
104. 455176.
105. 67725.
106. 707108.
107. 594342.
108. 56812.
109. 302399.
110. 482413.
111. 729904.
112. 482235.
113. 317225.
114. 133691.
115. 9429892.
116. 10990706.
117. 9929256.
118. 18098609.

Page 62.
6. $389.15.

7. $129.88.
8. $64.75.
9. $1573.66.
10. $2314.80.
11. $204.86.
12. $1949.92.
13. $318.30.
14. $2888.27.
15. $7177.89.
16. $2690.88.
17. $347.92.
18. $4660.94.
19. $2988.89.
20. $2224.99.
21. $774.97.
22. $302.75.
23. $3370.16.
24. $36549.91.
25. $279.47.

Page 74.
8. 6153.
9. 4152.
10. 6368.
11. 1428.
12. 2910.
13. 3642.
14. 2520.
15. 1472.
16. 3652.
17. 3714.
18. 1485.
19. 7704.
20. 6104.
21. 1813.
22. 2322.
23. 8586.
24. 3328.
25. 4832.
26. 1544.
27. 6615.
28. 4656.
29. 4200.
30. 2646.
31. 2403.
32. 780.
33. 1602.
34. 1228.

35. 2826.
36. 1503.
37. 3612.
38. 330.
39. 5776.
40. 996.
41. 34263.
42. 20426.
43. 38336.
44. 30348.
45. 37890.
46. 45270.
47. 16234.
48. 11844.
49. 635664.
50. 195545.
51. 153828.
52. 184724.
53. 159765.
54. 537672.
55. 327879.
56. 540228.
57. 5482442.
58. 2431092.
59. 892100.
60. 2369120.
61. 1969137.
62. 761394.
63. 2463208.
64. 2714715.
65. 2115141.
66. 1413714.
67. 4096365.
68. 772444.
69. 2999616.
70. 4554396.
71. 6188024.
72. 31205920.
73. 29100045.
74. 16001592.
75. 444800050.
76. 527662008.
77. 115563217.
78. 184554270.
79. 179556400.
80. 1000998333.
81. 2262624888.
82. 1978001250.

83. 3032424606.
84. 2333664666.
85. 4001503505.
86. 5402581380.
87. 5287192400.
88. 898500896.
89. 3600023139.
90. 3447941896.
91. 2430190616.
92. 6061510899.
93. 1443087780.
94. 6401605672.
95. 6916111029.
96. 2914871635.
97. 4051979262.
98. 6992046523.
99. 5239035168.
100. 7899262821.

Page 75.

6. 8416.
7. 8925.
8. 24660.
9. 7950.
10. 50858.

Page 76.

68. 2274520.
69. 6768256.
70. 4339392.
71. 34210026.
72. 11409475.
73. 19618774.
74. 29346660.
75. 17998952.
76. 17297524.
77. 36432067.
78. 10595270.
79. 42077502.
80. 13668578.
81. 22428029.
82. 87630160.
83. 55479270.
84. 13253889.
85. 319363968.
86. 466933275.
87. 2228718352.
88. 5851028272.

89. 4491013375.
90. 782579488998.
91. 508771409901.
92. 309659817705.
93. 449066450232.
94. 341297174372.
95. 535713688869.
96. 518811549053.
97. 890704248688.
98. 460251455490.
99. 459625992928.
100. 845234944685.
101. 593594835546.
102. 612483418296.
103. 455800781184.
104. 206174559600.
105. 157609964256.
106. 460614376508.
107. 366800407563.
108. 565561826817.
109. 398992848800.
110. 732830838375.
111. 180740630420.
112. 206067027144.
113. 708959004757.
114. 244781411316.
115. 521002778788.
116. 1828641592880.
117. 4126528054425.
118. 2417660129745.
119. 1947326108996.
120. 1907389937584.
121. 1054051915294.
122. 58474691616.
123. 3940221810.
124. 20276775525.
125. 204532557528.
126. 375045400048.
127. 469371849063.
128. 24243253994106.
129. 6520596662289.
130. 96656061072.
131. 180390783218.
132. 52491648826908.

Page 78.

3. 5670.
4. 98600.

5. 35900.
6. 262500.
7. 187400.
8. 76300.
9. 330000.
10. 266000.
11. 527400.
12. 243360.
13. 907320.
14. 3790550.
15. 1510560.
16. 3143160.
17. 221400.
18. 1021500.
19. 1536290.
20. 198660.
21. 1284000.
22. 28480000.
23. 32000000.
24. 29240000.
25. 13680000.
26. 88020000.
27. 128250000.
28. 390400000.
29. 141150000.
30. 551200000.
31. 1722200000.
32. 7452000000.
33. 802080000000.
34. 391950000000.
35. 52920000000.
36. 145800000000.
37. 512460000000.

Page 89.

6. 210.
7. 190.
8. 139.
9. 57.
10. 49.
11. 49.
12. 88.
13. 185.
14. 79.
15. 92.
16. 175, Rem. 4.
17. 64.
18. 118.

19. 312, Rem. 2.
20. 238, Rem. 1.
21. 210, Rem. 1.
22. 122.
23. 126.
24. 102, Rem. 4.
25. 44.
26. 80, Rem. 2.
27. 76, Rem. 3.
28. 67.
29. 62, Rem. 4.
30. 390, Rem. 5.
31. 1490, Rem. 5.
32. 268, Rem. 3.
33. 676, Rem. 8.
34. 1008, Rem. 6.
35. 1073, Rem. 1.
36. 1185, Rem. 1.
37. 1470.
38. 1459, Rem. 1.
39. 1334.
40. 1400.
41. 1285, Rem. 5.
42. 750.
43. 200, Rem. 1.
44. 425.
45. 1757, Rem. 2.
46. 397, Rem. 3.
47. 2453.
48. 947, Rem. 4.
49. 559, Rem. 1.
50. 823, Rem. 8.
51. 1333, Rem. 2.
52. 1336, Rem. 2.
53. 290.
54. 9188.
55. 2702, Rem. 1.
56. 6141, Rem. 2.
57. 4179.
58. 7109.
59. 31002, Rem. 1.
60. 17242, Rem. 4.
61. 5968, Rem. 8.
62. 12936.
63. 2684, Rem. 2.
64. 1391, Rem. 5.
65. 702, Rem. 4.
66. 720, Rem. 2.

67. 335.
68. 1644, Rem. 3.
69. 4345063, Rem. 7.
70. 5331567, Rem. 8.
71. 37326742, Rem. 1.
72. 12140168.
73. 11910500, Rem. 1.
74. 6233335.
75. 10048586.
        Rem. 7.
76. 3479302, Rem. 6.
77. 8571431, Rem. 6.
78. 19024270, Rem. 1.
79. 16650044, Rem. 1.
80. 4855279, Rem. 7.
81. 1563674115630,
        Rem. 1.
82. 8604700211872,
        Rem. 2.
83. 13125755354069,
        Rem. 1.
84. 2937509741427,
        Rem. 1.
85. 3956807481076,
        Rem. 4.
86. 6160278878046,
        Rem. 2.
87. 11226357885162,
        Rem. 1.
88. 3072737557048,
        Rem. 4.
89. 13270925528735.
90. 20042735065016,
        Rem. 3.
91. 133329622014677.
92. 8173791739972,
        Rem. 2.
93. 16242619728506,
        Rem. 3.
94. 11016672431296,
        Rem. 2.
95. 7031918938270,
        Rem. 2.
96. 6000000057525.
97. 6001141662520,
        Rem. 1.
98. 2583387790012,
        Rem. 3.

99. 13059466240519,
        Rem. 5.
100. 11401140013560.
101. 14156455244004,
        Rem. 5.
102. 8584902259705.
103. 1387502780556,
        Rem. 7.
104. 18196172130007,
        Rem. 4.

Page 92.

3. 24.
4. 18.
5. 39.
6. 19.
7. 28.
8. 42.
9. 12.
10. 22.
11. 16.
12. 11, Rem. 58.
13. 13.
14. 18, Rem. 7.
15. 10, Rem. 6.
16. 17.
17. 11, Rem. 31.
18. 12.
19. 12, Rem. 16.
20. 11, Rem. 10.
21. 9.
22. 19.
23. 14, Rem. 16.
24. 10, Rem. 20.
25. 10, Rem. 80.
26. 14, Rem. 9.
27. 86, Rem. 5.
28. 89.
29. 77.
30. 47.
31. 106, Rem. 36.
32. 102, Rem. 10.
33. 161, Rem. 14.
34. 38, Rem. 10.
35. 258.
36. 254, Rem. 7.
37. 96, Rem. 82.

38. 78.
39. 32, Rem. 47.
40. 165, Rem. 12
41. 38, Rem. 23.
42. 84, Rem. 8.
43. 38, Rem. 27.
44. 135, Rem. 9.
45. 102, Rem. 2.
46. 363, Rem. 14.
47. 184, Rem. 8.
48. 118, Rem. 32.
49. 111, Rem. 6.
50. 41, Rem. 23.
51. 68, Rem. 8.
52. 112, Rem. 48.
53. 11, Rem. 32.
54. 58, Rem. 56.
55. 272, Rem. 24.
56. 90, Rem. 70.
57. 312, Rem. 22.
58. 89, Rem. 14.
59. 197, Rem. 13.
60. 78, Rem. 30.
61. 88, Rem, 26.
62. 80, Rem, 60.
63. 728.
64. 1900, Rem. 8.
65. 891.
66. 317.
67. 892, Rem. 63.
68. 384, Rem, 21.
69. 3550, Rem. 22.
70. 2516, Rem. 36.
71. 763, Rem. 63.
72. 699, Rem. 5.
73. 3107, Rem. 26.
74. 2304, Rem. 26.
75. 255, Rem. 9.
76. 789, Rem. 62.
77. 923, Rem. 26.
78. 18791827272, Rem. 3.
79. 38491726580, Rem. 4.
80. 10792102382, Rem. 57.
81. 9763697554, Rem. 52.

82. 2286894574, Rem. 44.
83. 7384926150.
84. 1954833495, Rem. 6.
85. 8293746350, Rem. 2.
86. 3259432941, Rem. 27.
87. 1480583657, Rem. 45.
88. 10069725607, Rem. 4.
89. 27465236820, Rem. 18.
90. 5467398200, Rem. 18.
91. 7483926002, Rem. 9.
92. 6758394003, Rem. 37.
93. 9612081264, Rem. 67.
94. 586, Rem. 62.
95. 249, Rem. 77.
96. 129.
97. 73, Rem. 448.
98. 691, Rem. 42.
99. 97.
100. 166, Rem. 3.
101. 140.
102. 47, Rem. 84.
103. 242, Rem. 144.
104. 109, Rem. 167.
105. 31, Rem. 46.
106. 750, Rem. 469.
107. 1073, Rem. 449.
108. 1759, Rem. 406.
109. 912, Rem. 255.
110. 751, Rem. 274.
111. 1347, Rem. 527.
112. 942057, Rem. 106.
113. 836571, Rem. 137.
114. 80037, Rem. 40.

115. 3988458, Rem. 39.
116. 30013, Rem. 40.
117. 1954751, Rem. 230.
118. 1598129, Rem. 25.
119. 1326531, Rem. 52.
120. 1201803, Rem. 370.
121. 1072580, Rem. 37.
122. 140009, Rem. 714.
123. 558782, Rem. 500.
124. 2292341, Rem. 10.
125. 850539, Rem. 80.
126. 1020179, Rem. 598.
127. 2432441, Rem. 230.
128. 1225245, Rem. 132.
129. 2096720, Rem. 236.
130. 825921, Rem. 716.
131. 1395850, Rem. 427.
132. 552577, Rem. 192.
133. 775795, Rem. 471.
134. 753609, Rem. 297.
135. 2485911, Rem.' 225.
136. 3393573, Rem. 208.
137. 3866361, Rem. 164.
138. 368196, Rem. 345.

139. 473773,
     Rem. 247.
140. 1057028,
     Rem. 140.
141. 4211229,
     Rem. 27.
142. 3195376,
     Rem. 93.
143. 1740983,
     Rem. 129.
144. 1706223,
     Rem. 497.
145. 270765,
     Rem. 76.
146. 1124659,
     Rem. 638.
147. 774185, Rem. 232.
148. 71927024435,
     Rem. 100.
149. 165748654358,
     Rem. 66.
150. 8273945160.
151. 31873914029,
     Rem. 86.
152. 70230893142,
     Rem. 90.
153. 5957579763,
     Rem. 40.
154. 7384926537,
155. 35420573539,
     Rem. 148.
156. 382943812,
     Rem. 42.
157. 382947600,
     Rem. 15.

158. 468117558,
     Rem. 442.
159. 372849000,
     Rem. 196.
160. 718641765,
     Rem. 446.
161. 2180426148,
     Rem. 294.
162. 1108473674,
     Rem. 495.
163. 801961758,
     Rem. 498.
164. 862.
165. 401.
166. 1284,
     Rem. 4500.
167. 1112, Rem. 460.
168. 870, Rem. 510.
169. 1457,
     Rem. 3507.
170. 540.
171. 271.
172. 455.
173. 664.
174. 496.
175. 600.
176. 913.
177. 992.
178. 998.
179. 1942, Rem. 772.
180. 747.
181. 1510, Rem. 983.
182. 123408600,
     Rem. 12.
183. 60010040.

184. 40960052,
     Rem. 1120.
185. 106654539,
     Rem. 2175.
186. 389938174,
     Rem. 401.
187. 235401900,
     Rem. 1238.
188. 59450422,
     Rem. 3096.
189. 69325546,
     Rem. 2292.
190. 213032908,
     Rem. 3955.
191. 111061407,
     Rem. 4505.
192. 114303103,
     Rem. 2146.
193. 26493857.
194. 22410541921,
     Rem. 218665.
195. 1764264631.
196. 6473928506.
197. 3958472601.
198. 6947261536.
199. 5839264713.
200. 4362917583.
201. 5738492719.

Page 97.

3. 142 days.
4. 21120 steps.
10. 30 pounds.
11. 21147 acres.
$19.